Commentary on Insurance Law

COIL

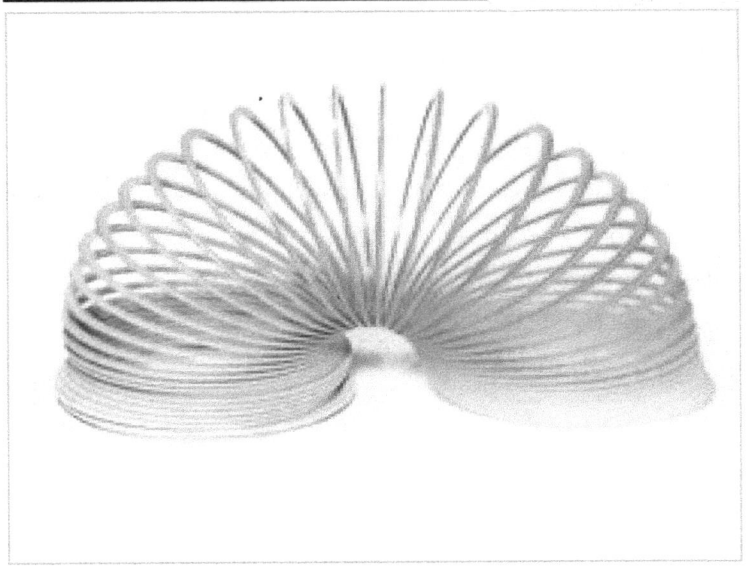

TABLE OF CONTENTS

Agent Who Kept Premium Owed to Zurich Loses at Ninth Circuit

Insurance agents, by contract with insurers they represent, must place all premium collected on behalf of the insurer and place the funds in a separate trust account. Depending on the terms of the contract the agent then deducts the agreed commission and remits the remainder to the insurer. Failure to remit the premium, less the commission, is a theft or conversion of funds to which the agent had no entitlement.

In *Zurich American Insurance Company v. Sealink Insurance Service Corp. And Yan Sara Zhang, and Phann Gelinda Keo, et al.*, No. 17-55776, United States Court of Appeals for the Ninth Circuit (October 15, 2018) Defendants Yan Sara Zhang and Sealink Insurance Service Corporation appealed from the district court's denial of their motion to set aside the entry of default and default judgment against them.

In evaluating such a motion, an appellate court must consider three factors:

I.   whether the party seeking to set aside the default engaged in culpable conduct that led to the default;

II.   whether it had no meritorious defense; or

III.   whether reopening the default judgment would prejudice the other party.

A finding that any one of these factors is true is sufficient reason for the district court to refuse to set aside the default.

The Ninth Circuit did not reach the issue of defendants' culpable conduct because defendants' lack of a meritorious defense was sufficient to justify the district court's refusal to set aside the default and default judgment. Defendants have no meritorious defense to

Zurich American Insurance Company's breach of contract claim.

The defendants point to the lack of a written agreement and argue that the contract at issue does not exist. However, they do not dispute that Sealink sold insurance policies issued by Zurich in exchange for Sealink's remittance of premiums, and there is ample evidence of an agreement governing that arrangement. Defendants offer no facts to dispute the existence of an agreement, and general objections to the existence of a contract are insufficient to satisfy the meritorious defense requirement.

Defendants also lack a meritorious defense to Zurich's breach of fiduciary duty claim. Defendants do not dispute that Sealink failed to maintain the premiums it owed Zurich in a segregated trust account as required by California Insurance Code sections 1733 and 1734. Defendants' argument that those provisions do not provide Zurich with a cause of action is mistaken. The Ninth Circuit concluded that a civil action will lie for damages proximately resulting from a licensee's breach of the fiduciary obligations imposed by sections 1733 and 1734.

Finally, defendants fail to assert a meritorious defense to the size of the default judgment award. The district court determined that the declaration of Zurich's legal collection specialist and the billing statement generated by Zurich constituted proof sufficient to support Zurich's requested damages. Defendants' challenge to the sufficiency and reliability of that evidence does not amount to a meritorious defense. A mere general denial regarding the extent of the deficiency owed is not enough to justify vacating a default or default judgment.

Defendants fail to offer specific facts disputing the damages amount despite being in the best position to have the accurate records required to refute Zurich's evidence. Defendants' assertion that they lack records substantiating the claimed amount does not amount to an allegation of "sufficient facts that, if true, would constitute a defense.

The district court did not err in failing to set aside the default judgment pursuant to Federal Rules of Civil Procedure that provides for relief when a judgment is void. In contrast to the other grounds for relief a default judgment may be vacated on this ground even if the defendant lacks a meritorious defense.

The defendants argued that the judgment is void due to inadequate service of process. But Zurich's service of process satisfied the statutory requirements. Zurich's substituted service of the summons and complaint on Zhang was proper. Zurich's service of the summons and complaint on Sealink complied with Federal Rules of Civil Procedure. Finally, Zurich served both Zhang and Sealink with its motion to enter default judgment in accordance with the Central District of California's Local Rules.

COIL Opinion

This case establishes that insurance fraud is not limited to people who are insured defrauding an insurer. In this case the insurer trusted the agents and allowed them to bind insurance with Zurich in exchange for a promise to remit premiums. Zurich was the victim of fraud by the agent and, rather than attempt a criminal prosecution for conversion, sued the agent and obtained a judgment which was upheld by the Ninth Circuit Court of Appeal. Zurich should execute on the judgment and obtain the full amount of the judgment. If not, it should seek prosecution of those who unlawfully converted Zurich's funds to their own use.

Asbestos Victim Fund Under Investigation

When a company is unable to pay liabilities related to asbestos exposure, it may file for Chapter 11 bankruptcy protection. Companies that successfully file are protected from lawsuits.

Asbestos companies are reviewed for bankruptcy reorganization under section 524(g) of the U.S. Bankruptcy Code. They attempt to fund trusts with enough money to pay current and future asbestos claims.

Companies establish the trusts, but trustees manage them and decide the amount of compensation paid to claimants.

In total, all asbestos bankruptcy trusts hold more than $30 billion. This figure comes from a 2016 report from RAND Corporation's Institute for Civil Justice.

These trusts have paid claimants approximately $18 billion since the late 1980s. This figure includes an estimated $15 billion from 2006 to 2012.

The U.S. Justice Department in the last two months of 2018 demanded trust documents as part of a civil investigation, opposed the creation of another trust it said lacked sufficient safeguards, and argued against the appointment of a lawyer it said was too conflicted to represent victims.

The actions take aim at a system that over decades has paid out billions of dollars to the sick and cancer-stricken, but that critics say is opaque and prone to fraud and manipulation by well-connected lawyers. The government's intervention aligns it with business groups who have long complained about the process.

But plaintiffs' lawyers and asbestos victims' advocates say there's scant proof of widespread fraud, particularly for a system that has accommodated millions of claims. And University at Buffalo law professor S. Todd Brown said the additional government oversight, while not a bad idea, "could lead to money going to complying with this oversight rather than going to the victims."

The trusts started emerging in the 1980s, formed by makers of asbestos-containing products who sought bankruptcy protection in the face of lawsuits from people who feared they had been exposed. The maneuvering enabled the companies to shield themselves from lawsuits while setting aside money to pay pending and future claims for asbestos, an environmental hazard once found in everyday products that can lead to the deadly mesothelioma cancer and other illnesses.

A 2011 Government Accountability Office report identified 60 trusts formed between 1988 and 2010 that it said had paid about 3.3 million claims valued at more than $17 billion.

Lawyers for asbestos victims say the process enables people to obtain compensation for catastrophic illness without drawn-out lawsuits.

Some claim that weak oversight allows people to collect payments with minimal evidence they were harmed by a particular company's product, and for illnesses far less serious than mesothelioma and lung cancer. They argue trust overseers are often tied to well-connected

plaintiffs' firms, raising concerns of favoritism and cronyism.

In 2014, a judge in the bankruptcy case of an asbestos gasket maker described a "startling pattern of misrepresentation" by alleged victims and their lawyers. The judge found that plaintiffs repeatedly told Garlock Sealing Technologies that it was responsible for their exposure and struck large settlement agreements with the company, only to later file claims with multiple other trusts over injuries and exposures they hadn't previously disclosed.

The Justice Department stepped up its oversight in the last few months.

In September, it challenged the creation of a new trust it said lacked details about how it would guard against fraud and abuse. The department said in a letter to state attorneys general that "it would object to plans for asbestos trusts that fail to include critical information on how asbestos claims will be evaluated, paid and reported" or that don't do enough to prevent fraud.

It later challenged a different corporation, Duro Dyne, over the appointment of a lawyer it said was too conflicted to represent the interests of people before the trust who may later become ill. A judge rejected that request, and Jeffrey Prol, an attorney for Duro Dyne, said he was taken aback by what he called the department's effort to make "this bankruptcy case a referendum on the asbestos trust system."

At least one trust, DII Industries, has disclosed receiving an administrative subpoena, to produce records of settlements as part of an investigation into whether Medicare is being properly reimbursed for trust payments. A trust spokesman said it was complying.

Business groups and defense lawyers contend weak oversight allows people to collect payments with minimal evidence they were harmed by a particular company's product, and for illnesses far less serious than mesothelioma and lung cancer. They argue trust overseers are often tied to well-connected plaintiffs' firms, raising concerns of favoritism and cronyism.

Justice Department Files Statement of Interest in New Asbestos Trust Proposal

The Department of Justice on September 13, 2018 filed a Statement of Interest in *In re Kaiser Gypsum Co.* in the United States Bankruptcy Court for the Western District of North Carolina. In the case, Kaiser Gypsum Company and Hanson Permanente Cement Inc. propose the establishment of a new asbestos trust under 11 U.S.C. § 524(g), a section of the Bankruptcy Code that provides the framework for responding to the unique issues associated with asbestos liability.

"In recent years, alarming evidence has emerged of fraud and mismanagement inside asbestos trusts," said Principal Deputy Associate Attorney General Jesse Panuccio. "Asbestos victims should feel certain that they will receive compensation when they are promised it, but fraudulent claims and mismanagement call that promise into question. In addition, the United States and all who depend on Medicare are harmed when Medicare is not reimbursed for treatment costs that have been paid by trust funds. With today's Statement of Interest, the Department sends a clear message that we will not tolerate fraudulent conduct that cheats asbestos victims and the United States. This is just one action the Department will take to increase the transparency and accountability of asbestos trusts, and we are grateful for the many partners we have in that mission, including the many state attorneys general who have brought attention to this issue. We encourage anyone with information about fraud or mismanagement of asbestos trusts to report it to the Department of Justice."

Congress enacted 11 U.S.C. § 524(g) to create a comprehensive mechanism for addressing injuries caused by asbestos. Under section 524(g) plans, asbestos-related claims may be channeled to a special trust created under the bankruptcy plan of reorganization, which then assumes responsibility for both the defense and payment of those claims. The trusts are managed by trustees, who often must secure support for major decisions from a "trust advisory committee" (TAC), whose members are often the same attorneys who represented asbestos claimants during the bankruptcy. Since 1994, more than 60 such trusts have been established by chapter 11 debtors with asbestos-related liabilities. According to the Government Accountability Office, asbestos bankruptcy trusts paid $17.5 billion from 1988 through 2011, and more recent studies estimate higher amounts.

In recent years, both courts and researchers have expressed growing concern that the trusts, enabled by a lack of oversight or accountability, may be paying fraudulent claims and mismanaging funds. In 2014, the same bankruptcy court in which the United States today filed its statement of interest found a substantial pattern of fraud in another case, In re Garlock Sealing Technologies, LLC, 504 B.R. 71 (Bankr. W.D.N.C. 2014). The court found that, in a sample of 15 civil asbestos cases, in each and every case key evidence about asbestos exposure had been improperly misrepresented or withheld. In three instances, plaintiffs made claims against defendants to whose products they had previously represented they had never been exposed. Similarly, several studies have demonstrated problems caused by the lack of oversight. One study found that, in the study period, people without malignant asbestos injury accounted for 86 percent of all claims made to the trusts and 37 percent of all trust payments. Another found that many of the claim forms submitted by the same claimants and law firms to different trusts contradicted each other. The secrecy with which many trust claims are submitted, allowed, and paid has made it nearly impossible to detect when plaintiffs are seeking a recovery based on misrepresentations.

The United States' Statement of Interest argues that the plans currently on file in this case do not have sufficient safeguards in place to prevent fraud and abuse. The Statement also indicates that the United States will object to any plan that lacks critical provisions to ensure transparency and accountability and to prevent fraudulent claims and mismanagement of the trust funds, including provisions: that require compliance with the Medicare Secondary Payer Statute; that notify claimants of their potential obligation to reimburse Medicare; that prevent excessive administrative costs and attorney contingency fees; that avoid conflicts of interest among members of the TAC; and that prevent payments to those who cannot demonstrate exposure to the defendants' products or who have made inconsistent claims in other asbestos proceedings. The United States is filing this Statement of Interest now to allow the parties sufficient time to address the concerns it raises.

Finally, in addition to filing the Statement of Interest, the Department also responded today to letters from 19 state attorneys general regarding concerns over asbestos trusts.

The Department will continue to look for opportunities to increase the transparency of asbestos trusts and protect the interests of legitimate claimants and the United States. The Department will also investigate conduct related to asbestos trusts that is illegal under federal law. If anyone has information on asbestos trust fraud or mismanagement, the Department welcomes the reporting of that information so that it may pursue all appropriate means under federal law to ensure that asbestos trusts operate lawfully and responsibly.

Until recently, the defense bar pointed to only a smattering of reported instances of the type of deception that my case so clearly illustrated. In contrast, opponents of reform continued to assert that systemic fraud did not exist—or at least had not been established—and the few examples.

The decision of the United States Bankruptcy Court for the Western District of North Carolina in *In re Garlock Sealing Techs., LLC.*, 504 B.R. 71 (Bankr. W.D. N.C., 2014) In re Garlock Sealing Techs., LLC., 504 B.R. 71 (Bankr. W.D. N.C., 2014) in gasket-manufacturer Garlock Sealing Technologies, Inc.'s estimation proceeding is certain to have silenced to some extent the zealousness with which plaintiffs and their attorneys have resisted transparency reforms. The *Garlock* opinion represents a stunning expose' of the breadth of the practice of withholding exposure evidence concerning the products of bankrupt entities. As is evident from the scope and detail of the opinion, the court in Garlock embarked on an extensive effort to understand fully the history of asbestos litigation in the United States, the scientific evidence relating to asbestos and asbestos-related disease, including epidemiology and industrial hygiene expert testimony, the social science relating to asbestos litigation practices, and its evolution into the dual compensation system that exists today. Undertaking this estimation effort, the court deviated from the usual practice of projecting the number of claims a trust anticipates receiving, and then determining the historic settlement value of those claims, so as to approximate what the trust's solvent predecessor would have paid to settle lawsuits. In so doing, Judge Hodges unearthed what can best be described as a stunning pattern of fraud and misrepresentation that should provide new and powerful support for the defense bar's crusade for greater openness.

Specifically, in order to estimate Garlock's liability for present and future mesothelioma claims relating to its asbestos-containing products, the Bankruptcy Judge authorized additional investigation to determine the legitimacy of using Garlock's settlement history as an accurate measure of its future liability. The evidence he found as a result of delving into the facts of only fifteen out of hundreds of settled cases resulted in the court's conclusion that "[i]t was a regular practice by many plaintiffs' firms to delay filing Trust claims for their clients so that remaining tort system defendants would not have that information." That finding also led to the court's scathing criticism "that the last ten years of [Garlock's] participation in the tort system was infected by the manipulation of exposure evidence by plaintiffs and their lawyers."

In its exhaustive historical review of the shifting nature of asbestos litigation since the early 2000s, when the large thermal insulation defendants were no longer subject to suit as a result of their bankruptcies, the court described in detail how the plaintiffs' attention turned to more peripheral defendants like Garlock, who were not producing the more toxic thermal insulation products, but manufacturing items like gaskets, some asbestos-containing.

Since this calculated withholding of evidence served to distort the level of responsibility on the part of Garlock and others, the court could not avoid reaching this disturbing judgment:

These fifteen cases are just a minute portion
of the thousands that were resolved by
Garlock in the tort system. . . . But, the fact
that *each and every one of them* contains such
demonstrable misrepresentation is surprising
and persuasive. . . . It appears certain that
more extensive discovery would show more
extensive abuse. But that is not necessary
because the startling pattern of
misrepresentations that has been shown is
sufficiently persuasive

Garlock's story is typical of many of the remaining
solvent codefendants in the asbestos tort system who
began being sued with increasing frequency beginning in
the early 1980s, despite the fact that the products they
sold exposed people to lower doses of a relatively less
potent chrysotile asbestos and almost always in the
context in which they were exposed to much higher
levels of more potent amphibole asbestos from
manufacturers who were no longer viable defendants in
the tort system. These more remote defendants
increasingly became lead defendants in the tort system,
resulting in elevated shares of liability, notwithstanding
that they, like Garlock, consistently maintained that their
products did not cause asbestos disease. Judge Hodges'
conclusions regarding the lower levels of toxicity of
chrysotile asbestos, and those of Garlock's products, are
significant because these are the factual findings of an
experienced judge, rather than the determination of a
jury.

If you do the Crime You Must Do the Time

Guilty of Disability Fraud

Insurance criminals today define the Yiddish word "Chutzpah!" Their unmitigated gall to challenge a conviction for fraud is without bound. They appeal and waste the time of courts of appeal. More often than not the attempt fails, even in the very liberal Ninth Circuit Court of Appeal.

In *United States Of America v. Jasvir Kaur, United States Of America, v. Harjit Johal,* No. 17-10306, No. 17-10307, United States Court Of Appeals For The Ninth Circuit (October 17, 2018) Harjit Kaur Johal and Jasvir Kaur challenge their convictions under 18 U.S.C. § 1623 for making false declarations to a grand jury during its investigation of a large-scale unemployment and disability insurance fraud scheme orchestrated by Mohammad Riaz "Ray" Khan and Mohammad Shabaz Khan.

DISCUSSION

The defendants argued that the joinder where they were both tried together was improper. The Ninth Circuit concluded that joinder was proper under Fed. R. Crim. P. 8(b) because, although Kaur and Johal were charged with separate counts of offering false testimony to the grand jury, the indictment stemmed from the same larger investigation and the false testimony related to the same aspects of the alleged fraudulent scheme.

The charges against each defendant arose out of the same series of acts or transactions and a substantial number of the facts the Government needed to prove at trial were overlapping. Moreover, even if they were improperly joined, reversal is not required because improper joinder is subject to harmless error review. Kaur and Johal have failed to show any possible prejudice.

Kaur and Johal argued that the district court improperly admitted evidence under Federal Rule of Evidence 404(b) that Johal participated in earlier fraud schemes organized by the Khan brothers. Even assuming the Government is incorrect that these prior acts fall outside the parameters of Rule 404(b) because they are inextricably intertwined with the charged offense, the evidence was properly admitted under Rule 404(b)(2) for the purpose of showing lack of mistake and a common plan or scheme. The court did not plainly err in failing to exclude the evidence under Federal Rule of Evidence 403. Moreover, even without the challenged evidence, the evidence against Kaur and Johal was overwhelming, so any error in the admission was harmless.

Whether Kaur and Johal actually picked peaches and whether they purchased pay stubs from Ray Khan were questions capable of influencing the grand jury investigation and therefore were material. And the questions posed to Kaur and Johal were not so ambiguous that their answers could be considered "literally true."

Finally, the Government presented sufficient evidence to support a jury finding that Kaur purchased pay stubs, even if the testimony of certain trial witnesses identifying her could be called into question. Because there was overwhelming independent evidence against the defendants any error in admitting the in-court identification testimony was harmless beyond a reasonable doubt.

The Sentencing Guidelines permit a three-level increase for substantial interference with the administration of justice if the defendant's perjury caused the unnecessary expenditure of substantial governmental or court resources. Although the underlying expenses associated with prosecuting Kaur for perjury cannot be included in this calculation the district court found that the Government expended other resources as a result of Kaur's perjury.

In light of the Government's representation that it called additional witnesses before the grand jury as a result of Kaur's perjury, and in light of evidence that it called Kaur to testify again after she was offered immunity, this determination was not clearly erroneous.

COIL OPINION

When people lie to a grand jury and are caught in the lie the government has no choice but to charge and convict them of perjury. The opinion made it clear that the crime was obvious and proved beyond a reasonable doubt. If there was any justice the two would have accepted the sentence and served their time. Rather, exercising unmitigated gall, they appealed.

When Reasonable Expectations are not Reasonable

When a Court Reads and Understands a Policy Justice is Done

Almost no one reads an insurance policy. Regardless, the words of the policy still control any question about coverage for a claim if they are clear and unambiguous.

Insureds are never happy when a claim is denied even if the decision to refuse defense and indemnity are clear, unambiguous and obvious. They sue and try to convince a court that the coverage should apply to the insured seeking coverage, usually by claiming the reasonable expectations doctrine applies since they can easily testify that they reasonably expected to have the coverage they needed. However, if a court allowed an insured to override the plain language of a policy limitation anytime he or she was dissatisfied with the limitation by simply invoking the reasonable expectations doctrine, the language of insurance policies would cease to have meaning and, as a consequence, insurers would be unable to project risk.

In *Frederick Mutual Insurance Co. v. Donald Hall, Individually And Trading As Hallstone, Inc.; Maria A. Hall, Individually And Trading As Hallstone, Inc.; Hallstone, Inc.; R. Lee Hulko; Bradley B. Fair*, No. 17-3477, United States Court Of Appeals For The Third Circuit (November 8, 2018) Plaintiff-Appellant Frederick Mutual Insurance Company ("Frederick") appealed the adverse decision of a trial court in a declaratory judgment action in which it sought to have the District Court declare that it did not have the duty to defend and indemnify Hailstone, Inc. ("Hailstone") under an insurance policy that Frederick issued to Hailstone in a state court action against Hailstone.

FACTUAL BACKGROUND

Donald and Marie Hall formed Hailstone to provide stone masonry work for residential premises. On the advice of a builder, Donald Hall ("Hall"), a principal in Hailstone, approached the Fraser Insurance Agency ("Fraser") to obtain an insurance policy to provide in Hall's words "maximum," "soup to nuts" coverage for Hailstone. Fraser obtained a liability policy from Frederick for Hailstone. Hall and Frederick did not have direct contact and Hall never asked for or received a copy of the policy Frederick issued.

Beginning in or around March 2006, R. Lee Hulko and Bradley B. Fair ("the Customers") contracted with Hailstone to provide custom stone masonry work for their home. The project was a substantial undertaking as it took several years to complete and the Customers paid nearly $300,000 for the project. The Customers discovered that some of the stone masonry work that Hailstone had undertaken had been damaged and required substantial repairs ultimately costing $352,294. The Customers attributed the damage to what they regarded was Hailstone's substandard and defective work and consequently they filed a state court action in Pennsylvania against Hailstone alleging breach of warranty, negligence, and related statutory claims.

While defending Hailstone in the state court action, Frederick filed this declaratory judgment action in the District Court, seeking a determination that it did not have a duty under its policy to defend and indemnify Hailstone for its defective workmanship. At the bench trial the Court found that the insurance policy unambiguously excluded faulty workmanship coverage.

Regardless the Court also found that Hall believed the policy provided coverage '" if something was done inadvertently', or if his business did something and someone made a claim against his business that he might be liable for," *Frederick Mut. Ins. Co. v. Hall*, No. 15-3354, 2017 WL 4883157, at *2 (E.D. Pa. Oct. 30, 2017). The Court's ultimate finding was that Hailstone had a reasonable expectation of workmanship coverage, and, accordingly, it entered judgment for Hailstone.

DISCUSSION

In reaching its decision, the District Court found that the insurance policy unambiguously excluded coverage for the faulty workmanship claims the Customers made in the underlying state court action, a conclusion with which the Third Circuit concurred.

It is well-settled that when policy language is unambiguous, a court must give effect to that language. It is also well-settled that the focus of any inquiry regarding issues of coverage under an insurance policy is the reasonable expectations of the insured. An insured, however, may not complain that its reasonable expectations have been frustrated when the applicable policy limitations are clear and unambiguous.

Having found the policy unambiguous, the Third Circuit concluded that the trial Court should have entered judgment for Frederick instead of applying the reasonable expectations doctrine.

Hall, however, did not apply for the specific type of insurance coverage he now claims that he expected. Rather, he asked in general terms for "soup to nuts" coverage. Although the request was broad it was not specific. Thus, Frederick could regard Hall's application for insurance as seeking a general liability insurance policy.

However, a general liability policy does not provide a guarantee of the policyholder's workmanship. A businessman purchases a liability insurance policy to transfer the risk and cost of unexpected and unintended happenings (occurrences) to his insurance company. The insurer only agrees to assume that risk for a calculated premium. The insurer does not, however, provide a guarantee of the businessman's workmanship or his products for that premium. Typically, the insurer protects itself against such claims by excluding coverage for property in the care, custody or control of the insured or property as to which the insured for any purpose is exercising control. There is usually some form of insurance available to cover injury to or destruction of the excluded property at a higher premium which is commensurate with the risk.

At no point did Hallstone specify that it desired the costlier workmanship insurance. An insured's failure to request or bargain for a particular coverage precludes a court from finding that the insured expected such coverage, whether or not the insured received a copy of the policy.

Pennsylvania case law makes clear that the District Court's application of the reasonable expectations doctrine was flawed. Only objectively reasonable expectations are protected. Hall's claim that he expected Hallstone's "maximum," "soup to nuts" liability policy to include workmanship coverage is no more reasonable than if a purchaser of auto insurance expected his policy to cover repairs if his car breaks down, even if he asked for "soup to nuts" coverage. It is simply not the kind of coverage insurance agents and insurance companies expect to provide unless the insured explicitly requests such coverage.

The Third Circuit refused to allow an insured to override the plain language of a policy limitation just because he or she was dissatisfied with the limitation by invoking the reasonable expectations doctrine. The language of insurance policies would cease to have meaning.

The Third Circuit refused, therefore, to set such a deleterious sequence of events into motion. Accordingly, it reversed the District Court's judgment and remanded the matter to that Court to enter judgment for Frederick.

ZALMA OPINION

In essence, the Third Circuit found that the hindsight expectations of the insured, Hallstone, which only arose after it was sued, were not reasonable in light of the clear and unambiguous language of the policy. Insurers are entitled to rely on the clear and unambiguous language of the policy agreed to by the insured before a loss. A court, in a declaratory judgment action is charged with interpreting the policy not rewriting it to meet what the insured learned it needed only after it was sued.

The Stupidity of Covering Others for More than Yourself

You Can't Make an Insurer Pay for Coverage You Didn't Buy

People injured in auto accidents usually have buyer's remorse about the insurance they purchased to protect themselves – like Uninsured Motorist/Underinsured Motorist (UM/UIM) coverage. Because the person is injured and needs money, he or she has no qualms about suing the insurance company to get the insurance coverage needed rather than the insurance coverage purchased.

New Jersey's appellate courts were faced with the coverage issues in *Christopher Cox v. Krystal Tomasso, NJM Insurance Group, And/Or New Jersey Reinsurance Group, And New Jersey Manufacturers Insurance Company*, Docket No. A-0106-17T2, Superior Court Of New Jersey Appellate Division (November 1, 2018) where Cox appealed an order granting summary judgment in favor of New Jersey Manufacturers Insurance Company (NJM).

FACTS

Plaintiff was injured when a car driven by Krystal Tomasso struck the motorcycle he was riding. Plaintiff had insured his motorcycle through Rider Insurance Company (Rider) under a policy with a $15,000 liability limit, which was $10,000 less than the $25,000 limit Tomasso had on her car. Thus, Tomasso's vehicle was not underinsured compared to the coverage on plaintiff's motorcycle.

Plaintiff sought underinsured motorist (UIM) benefits under a $500,000-limit policy he had obtained from NJM to cover his pick-up truck.

THE POLICY

The liability section of the NJM policy specifically stated that NJM did not provide liability coverage for "the ownership, maintenance or use" of any vehicle with fewer than four wheels. NJM did not provide liability coverage for plaintiff's motorcycle or for plaintiff while he was riding a motorcycle. Therefore, he obtained a separate policy from Rider to cover his motorcycle.

The UIM section of the NJM policy explicitly excluded coverage for plaintiff "[w]hile occupying any vehicle insured by another motor vehicle policy in which you or a family member are a named insured." That provision further stated: "However, this exclusion . . . does not affect UM/UIM coverage for minimum limits required by New Jersey law for liability coverage.

NJM denied plaintiff's UIM claim on the basis of this exclusion because he was the named insured on the Rider motorcycle policy and Tomasso's vehicle had limits higher than the $15,000 minimum required by law.

The trial judge granted NJM summary judgment, reasoning that the policy exclusion was unambiguous and was clearly applicable to plaintiff's situation. The trial judge rejected plaintiff's argument that the NJM Buyer's Guide created an ambiguity in the policy.

ANALYSIS

When a court construes an insurance policy it must recognize that insurance policies are contracts of adhesion drafted by experts but read by consumers who are lay persons. Accordingly, the court will attempt to give effect to the insured's reasonable expectations and construe genuinely ambiguous clauses favorably to the insured. Nonetheless, an insurance policy that is clear and unambiguous should be enforced as written. If the policy's plain language is unambiguous, the court may not engage in a strained construction to support the imposition of liability or write a better policy for the insured than the one purchased.

The appellate court agreed with the trial judge that the NJM policy was not genuinely ambiguous, and the trial judge's interpretation of the policy is consistent with the insured's reasonable expectations.

Unlike the policy provision in a case cited by the plaintiff the NJM exclusion began with a complete sentence clearly stating a general exclusion. A reasonable reader would understand the exclusion as meaning that if, as here, he had insured a vehicle with another insurance company and was a named insured on that policy, NJM would not provide UIM coverage for the use of that vehicle. In that context, the second sentence, stating an exception to the exclusion, for "minimum" limits required by law, would not lead a reasonable reader to believe that NJM would provide $500,000 in UIM coverage for the use of such a vehicle.

Moreover, it should have come as no surprise to plaintiff that NJM would not provide UIM coverage when he was riding a motorcycle for which he had purchased separate coverage from another insurer, particularly when the NJM policy explicitly stated that it did not cover vehicles with fewer than four wheels (e.g., motorcycles).

While the result here is required by public policy, as opposed to the clear wording of the clause, it is consistent with the purpose of the UIM statute. That statute limits the purchase of UIM coverage to the amount of liability insurance the insured has purchased. Thus, an insured can obtain more UIM coverage by buying more liability insurance. This provides greater protection for both the insured and anyone the insured injures with his or her vehicle.

By buying only a minimum-liability policy for his motorcycle, which was his only liability coverage for that vehicle, plaintiff provided only $15,000 in liability protection for himself and in potential financial recovery for anyone he injured with his motorcycle. The court found no violation of public policy by limiting plaintiff to UIM coverage equal to the liability insurance he purchased for the motorcycle.

The insured got into an accident while riding his motorcycle, and Universal claimed that NJM should contribute to his UIM coverage. As here, the liability section of the NJM policy excluded liability coverage for motorcycles, i.e., for motorized vehicles with fewer than four wheels.

The NJM policy in this case has an unambiguous exclusion for situations where the insured is using a vehicle he owns, on which he is the named insured on another insurance policy. For that reason, plaintiff's argument that UIM coverage is linked to the injured person, not the covered vehicle, is unavailing. In this case, the policy language specifically excludes UIM coverage to the injured person, albeit based on his use of a vehicle which he insured under a separate policy.

ZALMA OPINION

States, for reasons known only to their legislators, set minimum liability limits to a paltry $15,000. Insurers, for reasonable premium, are willing to issue policies for higher policy limits up to multiple millions for both liability and UM/UIM coverages. Mr. Cox insured his pickup truck with $500,000 limits but decided to only take the minimum statutory limits for his motorcycle. As a result, he limited his recovery by choice and for saving a few dollars in premium he lost the ability to receive $500,000 in UIM coverage.

Appraisers Can't Determine Amount Without First Determining Cause of Loss

First Party Insurance Appraisers & Causation

Insurance appraisals are limited to a determination of the amount of loss. Some courts find that the cause of a loss is prohibited by the language of the appraisal provision of the policy since it limits the appraisers to a determination of the amount of loss and causation must be left to the courts. Others conclude that an appraisal must determine the cause before it can calculate the amount of loss.

In *Walnut Creek Townhome Association vs. Depositors Insurance Company,* In The Supreme Court Of Iowa, No. 16–0121 (August 10, 2018) the Supreme Court of Iowa was asked to determine if the trial court erred by rejecting an insurance appraisal award for hail damage to roofing shingles. The case presented a question of first impression in Iowa that has divided the courts of other jurisdictions: whether the appraisers may determine the CAUSE of the loss.

FACTS

The insured townhome association was already investigating a warranty claim against the manufacturer seeking replacement of allegedly defective shingles when the hailstorm occurred. The property insurer paid for damage to metal gutters and fascia but disputed whether the hail caused damage to the asphalt shingles and denied coverage based on the preexisting manufacturing defect. The Association sued the insurer for breach of contract and invoked the appraisal provision of the property insurance policy to ascertain the amount of the loss from the hailstorm. The appraisal panel considered conflicting expert opinions and, in a two-to-one decision, valued the hail-damage loss at approximately $1.4 million. The district court held a bench trial, rejected the appraisal award, found no shingle damage from hail, applied an exclusion for defective materials, and entered judgment in favor of the insurer.

The court of appeals held the district court erred by rejecting the appraisal award for shingle damage and remanded for entry of judgment on the appraisal award, excluding amounts for air conditioners not owned by the insured. A dissenting judge would have affirmed the district court judgment against the insured, concluding the district court was not bound by the appraiser's determination of the cause of the loss.

Walnut Creek Townhome Association (Walnut Creek or the Association) is a residential common interest community in Urbandale. The thirty-six multifamily buildings at Walnut Creek were built between 2004 and 2006. the board learned that the type of shingle used on its roofs — New Horizon manufactured by CertainTeed — was regarded by roofing professionals to be defective.

On August 8, 2012, a severe wind and hailstorm hit Walnut Creek. One resident described the hail as "pea size" and "dime size" and noted that it covered his entire deck.

In September, Walnut Creek asked Nicholas Waterman, a roofing renovator with GreenGuard Construction, to inspect the roofs for hail damage. Waterman found between eight to twelve hits per ten-by-ten-foot square and concluded that "[t]he roofing definitely had hail damage."

Walnut Creek is insured by Depositors Insurance Company (Depositors). Walnut Creek submitted an insurance claim to Depositors, alleging that the August 8 storm caused damage to the roofs, gutters, siding, soffits, and air conditioning units and that the policy covered such damage.

Walnut Creek and Depositors each named an appraiser, and their appraisers selected an umpire. Before the appraisal occurred, Walnut Creek filed a civil action against Depositors in district court for breach of contract and sought a declaratory judgment "that the appraisal award form specify the amount of the covered loss."

The appraisal took place on May 5, 2015. The appraisers inspected five buildings. The appraisal award stated:

> The appraisers and umpire above-referenced hereby agree and stipulate that the appraisal herein is limited in scope to the amount of loss and damage *as a result of a hail and windstorm that occurred on or about august 8, 2012*. The award does not include an evaluation or determination of coverage, policy exclusions or the relative causation of the same. (emphasis added)

The appraisal award set the amount of loss at $1,467,830.2. This included the replacement cost of the air conditioners, which the court later determined did not belong to Walnut Creek and, therefore, were not covered by the policy.

TRIAL COURT DECISION

The trial court concluded that Depositors did not breach the contract because the policy did not cover the damage to Walnut Creek's roofs. The court determined that the policy excludes coverage of the roof damage because

1. Walnut Creek did not prove the storm was the only cause of the physical damage to the roofs,

2. Walnut Creek did not disprove Depositors' contention that the shingles contained a product defect that triggered deterioration, and

3. The defective shingles were used in the construction of the townhomes even though the defect was well-known in the roofing industry.

The district court found that the damage to the shingles resulted from multiple concurrent causes, including the preexisting defect in the shingles; Walnut Creek was aware of the policy exclusions; and the appraisal, which was not signed by all parties, only addressed one of the causes of roof damage. The court concluded that Walnut Creek did not meet its burden of showing the appraisal award was binding and conclusive on the parties. The court denied Walnut Creek's breach of contract claim and claim for declaratory judgment.

ANALYSIS

The court is to decide coverage questions, but the appraisers' determination of the factual cause and monetary amount of the insured loss is binding on the parties absent fraud or other grounds to overcome a presumption of validity.

Since the state standard policy must be followed to the extent the final sentence of Depositors' appraisal provision purports to change the meaning of the provision, it is unenforceable.

Appraisal awards do not provide a formal judgment and may be set aside by a court. The appraisal award will not be set aside unless the complaining party shows fraud, mistake or misfeasance on the part of an appraiser or umpire.

Whether Causation Determinations Made by the Appraisal Panel Are Binding.

Depositors contends the district court was free to disregard the appraisal award in determining the cause of the shingle damage and in applying coverage exclusions for defective shingles. Coverage questions are for the court. But factual causation issues may be decided through the appraisal process. The appraisal award is presumptively binding on the parties and court.

The fighting issue here is whether the appraisers may determine the cause-in-fact of damage to insured property (here, roofing shingles) when appraising the amount of the loss from the hailstorm. Courts across the country are divided as to whether, in determining the 'amount of loss' pursuant to appraisal provisions like the one here, appraisers may consider questions of causation. Some courts view causation questions as off-limits for appraisers.

HOW LOSS IS DETERMINED

It would be extraordinarily difficult, if not impossible, for an appraiser to determine the amount of storm damage without addressing the demarcation between 'storm damage' and 'non-storm damage.' To hold otherwise would be to say that an appraisal is never in order unless there is only one conceivable cause of damage — for example, to insist that 'appraisals can never assess hail damage unless a roof is brand new. Under the circumstances of this case a determination of amount of loss under the appraisal clause includes a determination of causation. In Iowa, therefore, appraisers may decide the factual cause of damage to property in determining the amount of the loss from a storm.

Here, the appraisers themselves made clear they were determining only the amount of loss attributable to the hailstorm without deciding coverage exclusions or other causes of shingle damage.

Depositors' policy excludes coverage for preexisting deterioration caused by defective shingles. But the appraisers necessarily distinguished the hailstorm damage from deterioration of defective shingles installed between 2004 and 2006.

The Supreme Court concluded Depositors failed to overcome the appraisal award's presumption of validity.

On remand, the trial court was ordered to accept the appraisal award as to the hail damage loss, and then determine the amount, if any, Depositors owes under the policy after adjudicating the coverage defenses.

ZALMA OPINION

I have served as an appraiser in the past. It is impossible – especially when multiple causes of damage may exist – to set an amount of loss and damage without first determining causation. The appraisers in this case were wise enough to make clear in their award that it only determined the amount of hail damage and nothing more. The issue of coverage for damage to things like air conditioning was left to the trial court. Logic, in this case, won over legalistic sophistry.

Ethical Behavior & Success

To understand the connection between ethics and quality service, it is important to understand the meaning of ethical values in the insurance context. The ethical insurer and its ethical claims and underwriting staff must treat the insureds and claimants with whom they come in contact honestly, fairly and with utmost good faith. The contact must reflect the highest integrity, respect and empathy for the people who need the service of the insurer.

Finally, the insurer must reflect a high level of trustworthiness, fairness; honesty and personal accountability. Vince Lombardi reportedly said

> The quality of a person's life is in direct proportion to their commitment to excellence, regardless of their chosen field of endeavor.

The statement applies equally to football – about which Lombardi was speaking – and insurance. Excellence in the organization depends on the high ethical values and excellence in keeping the promises made by an insurance policy by the insurer's employees and officers.

Without excellence in claims handling and underwriting coupled with ethical behavior and conduct, an insurer will almost certainly fail. The insurer that demands excellence in claims handling and underwriting within the confines of ethical conduct and values will invariably succeed.

Attempts to Compel Ethical Behavior

Some states have attempted to compel insurers to act ethically and in good faith because of a perception that insurers were not treating the public fairly.

Most Bar Association ethics committees and courts hold that the employment relationship does not, in and of itself, constitute a violation of the professional duties of attorneys. The Missouri Supreme Court has held that there is no difference between a corporation doing something through an employee or through an independent contractor.[1]

An American Bar Association formal opinion states that the insurance company's obligation to defend an action brought by a third person against the insured contemplates that the company will take charge of the defense, including the supervision of the litigation. The essential point of ethics involved is that the lawyer so employed shall represent the insured as his client with undivided fidelity.[2]

---

[1] In Re: Allstate Insurance Co., 722 S.W.2d 947 (Mo.1987).

[2] ABA Comm. on Professional Ethics and Grievances, Formal Op. 282, p. 623 (1950).

The California Insurance Code contains a Fair Claims Practices statute that sets out multiple acts that the Legislature considered unethical and an unfair claims practice, including:

> (h) Knowingly committing or performing with such frequency as to indicate a general business practice any of the following unfair claims settlement practices:

> (1) Misrepresenting to claimants pertinent facts or insurance policy provisions relating to any coverages at issue.

> (2) Failing to acknowledge and act reasonably promptly upon communications with respect to claims arising under insurance policies.

> (3) Failing to adopt and implement reasonable standards for the prompt investigation and processing of claims arising under insurance policies.

> (4) Failing to affirm or deny coverage of claims within a reasonable time after proof of loss requirements have been completed and submitted by the insured.

> (5) Not attempting in good faith to effectuate prompt, fair, and equitable settlements of claims in which liability has become reasonably clear.

> (6) Compelling insureds to institute litigation to recover amounts due under an insurance policy by offering substantially less than the amounts ultimately recovered in actions brought by the insureds, when

the insureds have made claims for amounts reasonably similar to the amounts ultimately recovered.

(7) Attempting to settle a claim by an insured for less than the amount to which a reasonable person would have believed he or she was entitled by reference to written or printed advertising material accompanying or made part of an application.

(8) Attempting to settle claims on the basis of an application which was altered without notice to, or knowledge or consent of, the insured, his or her representative, agent, or broker.

(9) Failing, after payment of a claim, to inform insureds or beneficiaries, upon request by them, of the coverage under which payment has been made.

(10) Making known to insureds or claimants a practice of the insurer of appealing from arbitration awards in favor of insureds or claimants for the purpose of compelling them to accept settlements or compromises less than the amount awarded in arbitration.

(11) Delaying the investigation or payment of claims by requiring an insured, claimant, or the physician of either, to submit a preliminary claim report, and then requiring the subsequent submission of formal proof of loss forms, both of which submissions contain substantially the same information.

(12) Failing to settle claims promptly, where liability has become apparent, under one portion of the insurance policy coverage in order to influence settlements under other portions of the insurance policy coverage.

(13) Failing to provide promptly a reasonable explanation of the basis relied on in the insurance policy, in relation to the facts or applicable law, for the denial of a claim or for the offer of a compromise settlement.

(14) Directly advising a claimant not to obtain the services of an attorney.

(15) Misleading a claimant as to the applicable statute of limitations.[3]

The statute is enforced by the California Department of Insurance with fines and even a potential loss of the right to do business in the state. Violation of the statute can also be used at trial of a civil action to show a failure of the insurer to apply minimum standards of good faith and fair dealing and allow the trier of fact to impose tort damages on an insurer for the tort of bad faith and even assess punitive and exemplary damages.

Similar statutes have been enacted in most states. They establish a series of actions that the state considers unfair claims handling standards. Each state sets out different unfair acts some more than California and most less than California. All are attempts at establishing ethical conduct for insurers when presented with claims from insureds.

Ethics for Independent Insurance Adjusters

[3] California Insurance Code Section 790.03(h).

Independent insurance adjusters serve insurance companies who do not have sufficient claims staff to handle insurance claims on behalf of various insurers.

The professional insurance adjuster recognizes that the work of adjusting insurance claims is a profession of public trust. Independent insurance adjusters should maintain a standard of integrity that will promote the goal of building public confidence and trust in the insurance industry.

Independent insurance adjusters, and company employed insurance adjusters, should follow the following rules and standards of conduct:

- Adjusters should discharge claims responsibilities for which they possess sufficient technical competence or can acquire adequate training.

- Adjusters should seek only information they believe to be relevant, timely and accurate.

- Adjusters should use only legal and ethical means of obtaining information.

- Adjusters should handle claims with no intent to mislead or misinform.

- Adjusters should be sensitive to rights of individuals to privacy.

- Respecting the right of privacy, the adjuster will take reasonable measures to protect sensitive information from illegal or unauthorized examination.

- Adjusters should avoid illegal discrimination.

- Adjusters should strive to keep personal feelings and prejudices from influencing their judgment.

• Adjusters should maintain a courteous and sensitive attitude in their interactions with insureds and claimants, seeking to understand their concerns during times of distress.

• Adjusters should assist insureds in presenting and documenting their losses, and will not place the interests of the insurer above those of the insured.

• Adjusters should maintain their business relationships with others in a manner that will promote the goal of bringing credit and honor to the profession.

• Adjusters should have no undisclosed financial interest in any direct or indirect aspect of an adjusting transaction.

• Adjusters should obey the laws and regulations related to handling claims.

• Adjusters should resist fraudulent, unmeritorious or exaggerated claims, and support public and industry organizations involved in the detection and prevention of insurance fraud.

• Adjusters should seek out all available alternatives to litigation to resolve issues in an expeditious and conciliatory manner.

• Adjusters should approach investigations and adjustments with an unprejudiced and open mind and a determination to be fair with insured and insurer.

• Adjusters should make truthful and unbiased reports of facts as discovered.

• Adjusters should assume an unvarying attitude of fairness and by competence, integrity and respect for the person with whom they deal, to promote goodwill toward the business of insurance.

- Adjusters should resist influence tending to promote improper and extravagant settlements.

- Adjusters should avoid improper alliances.

- Adjusters should refrain from improper solicitation of business.

- Adjusters should be alert to changes in policy forms and methods in order to render the highest quality of service.

- Adjusters should work for economy of expense and equitable bills for service.

- Adjusters should serve the business of insurance with loyalty and cooperate with insurers and their designated representatives in the proper handling of claims and losses.

- Adjusters should work in harmony with one another and their clients so as to foster cordial relationships among themselves and with the insurance fraternity.[4]

In Canada, the following Code of Ethics has been adopted by statute:

> Code of ethics of claims adjusters An Act respecting the distribution of financial products and services (R.S.Q., c. D-9.2, s. 202.1, par. 1 and s. 312)

> DIVISION I

> GENERAL

[4] Adapted from the code of ethics of the Association of Registered Professional Adjusters [http://www.rpa-adjuster.com/ethics.html] and the California Association of Independent Insurance Adjusters [http://caiia.com/index.php?about.html]

1. The purpose of the provisions of this Code is to promote the protection of the public and the honest and competent practice of the professional activities of claims adjusters, regardless of the structure of their practice, the nature of their contractual relationship with clients or the class of the claims adjustment sector in which they practice.

2. Claims adjusters must ensure that they and their mandataries and employees comply with the provisions of the Act respecting the distribution of financial products and services (R.S.Q., c. D-9.2) and its regulations.

3. Claims adjusters must not, directly or indirectly, pay or promise to pay remuneration, compensation or any other benefit to a person who is not a representative in order for that person to act in that capacity or use that title.

4. Claims adjusters must not, directly or indirectly, procure a promise of payment or payment of remuneration, compensation or any other benefit from a person who is not a representative and who acts or attempts to act in that capacity.

5. Claims adjusters must not, directly or indirectly, procure a promise of payment or payment of remuneration, compensation or any other benefit not authorized by the Act or its regulations from a person other than the person who has retained their services.

6. Claims adjusters must not pay, offer to pay or agree to pay any remuneration, compensation or benefit to a person who is not a representative, except where permitted by law.

7. Claims adjusters must not pay or promise to pay any remuneration, compensation or benefit in order to have their professional services retained, except as provided by the Act or its regulations.

8. Claims adjusters must not accept, other than the remuneration or compensation to which they are entitled, any benefit relating to their professional activities, except where permitted by law.

9. Claims adjusters must avoid placing themselves, directly or indirectly, in a situation of conflict of interest. Without limiting the generality of the foregoing, a claims adjuster would be in a situation of conflict of interest where the interests involved are such that the claims adjuster may tend to favour certain interests over those of the client, or the claims adjuster's judgment and loyalty towards the client may be adversely affected; or the claims adjuster obtains a current or future personal benefit, directly or indirectly, for a particular act.

* * *

11. Claims adjusters must not

(1) have a personal interest in the settlement of a claim; (2) derive or seek to derive personal benefit from a matter

entrusted to them, other than their remuneration; (3) ask anyone, except a client or client's representatives, to inform them of an event giving rise to a claim; (4) obtain or attempt to obtain details concerning an insurance policy from any person other than a client or client's representatives, with a view to having the settlement of claim entrusted to them; or (5)   advise an insured, a claimant, a client or a third party against consulting another representative or another person of their choice.

* * *

15. The conduct of claims adjusters must be characterized by objectivity, discretion, moderation and dignity.

16. No claims adjuster may, in any manner whatsoever, make any representations that are false, misleading or likely to be misleading.

17. In their professional activities, claims adjusters must identify themselves clearly and, where applicable, identify their client. Claims adjusters must show their certificate upon request.

* * *

21. Claims adjusters must provide the insured with the explanations necessary for them to understand the settlement of the claim and services rendered to them.
* * *

25. Claims adjusters must avoid any misrepresentations as to their level of competence or the effectiveness of their services or those of their firm or independent partnership.

* * *

26. Before accepting a mandate, claims adjusters must take into account the limits of their abilities and knowledge and the means available to them. They must not undertake or continue a mandate for which they are not sufficiently prepared, without obtaining the necessary assistance.

27. Claims adjusters must act promptly, honestly and fairly in providing their professional services under the mandates entrusted to them.

* * *

34. Claims adjusters must submit every offer of settlement to the client.

* * *

38. Claims adjusters must not, through fraud, trickery or other deceitful means, avoid or attempt to avoid their professional civil liability or that of the firm or independent partnership within which they carry on their professional activities.

* * *

48. Claims adjusters must not mislead an insurer, abuse its good faith or use unfair practices in their dealings with the insurer.

49. Claims adjusters must not misrepresent to an insurer that they are responsible for settling a claim.

* * *

58. Acts by claims adjusters that are contrary to the honour and dignity of the profession constitute a breach of the Code of ethics, including (1) carrying on their professional activities dishonestly or negligently; (2) carrying on their professional activities under conditions or in situations likely to compromise the quality of services; (3) taking into account any intervention by a third party that could affect the performance of their professional duties to the detriment of the client or the insured; (4) knowingly deriving benefit from perjury or false evidence; (5) knowingly making a statement that is false, misleading or likely to be misleading; (6) participating in the preparation or preservation of evidence that they know is false; (7) paying or offering to pay a witness compensation conditional on the content of the witness's testimony or on the outcome of a case; (8) unduly withholding, concealing, harbouring, falsifying, mutilating or destroying evidence, whether directly or indirectly; (9) suppressing evidence that they have or a client has a legal obligation to preserve, disclose or produce; (10) concealing or

knowingly withholding that which a legislative or regulatory provision requires them to disclose; (11) advising or encouraging a client to commit an act that they know is illegal or fraudulent; (12) not informing the client, the insured or the opposing party of any impediment to the continuation of their mandate; (13) insistently or repeatedly urging a person to use their professional services; (14) carrying on their activities with persons not authorized by the Act or its regulations to carry on such activities or using their services to do so; charging for professional services not rendered or falsely described; and using or appropriating, for personal purposes, money or securities entrusted to them in the performance of any mandate, whether the activities carried on by them are in the sector of claims adjustment or in another sector governed by the Act.[5]

The professional insurance adjuster follows standards like those stated above to maintain the quality of the profession and to deal with insurance claims ethically and in good faith. Often the insurer's adjuster is asked to deal with a Public Insurance Adjuster who acts as the adjuster for the insured as the independent adjuster or company adjuster acts for the insurer.

The contact between the two should be professional and ethical. Rarely the contact between the professional adjuster and the public insurance adjuster is adversarial.

---

[5]   The full statute is available at
http://www2.publicationsduquebec.gouv.qc.ca/dynamicSearch/telecharge.php?type=3&file=/D_9_2/D9_2R1_02_1_A.HTM; you might also read the Florida adjuster's code of ethics available at
http://www.geocities.com/marthabees/adjustercode.html#anchor37407 .

Both should be working toward the same goal, the payment of proper and complete indemnity to the insured.

In Oklahoma, it was found that a disbarred or suspended lawyer needed to be prohibited from negotiating insurance claim settlements, including but not limited to, as a private insurance adjuster.[6] The court concluded that the disbarment took the lawyer out of the ability to treat an insured with the utmost good faith and refused to issue a license as a public insurance adjuster.

In Florida, unprofessional conduct of attorney occurring during his employment as an insurance adjuster and not as a practicing attorney nevertheless warranted his disbarment.[7]

The bar should conduct its own investigations, and the energy at the disposal of the Association of Casualty and Surety Companies might better be utilized in perfecting a code of ethics for insurance adjusters and in enforcing it, in as much as it is a matter of common knowledge, that activities of certain adjusters tend to breed the sort of unprofessional conduct alleged in the complaint filed in *Schoolfield v. Bean*, 26 Tenn.App. 30, 167 S.W.2d 359 and *State ex rel. Turner v. Denman*, 36 Tenn.App. 613, 259 S.W.2d 891.

---

[6] *In re Reinstatement of Blake*, 371 P.3d 465, 2016 OK 33 (2016)

[7] *State ex rel Florida Bar v. Clements*, 131 So.2d 198 (1961)

Rescission – the Equitable Remedy

Since, the Eighteenth Century insurance has been considered a business of the utmost good faith.

Parties to an insurance contract are required to deal with each other fairly and in good faith. Neither party should conceal any material facts from the other nor should either misrepresent any facts material to the decision to insure or not insure.

After 1935, if a California contract of insurance was entered into as a result of mistake of fact, mistake of law, concealment of material fact or misrepresentation of material fact the insurer or the insured has the right to rescind the policy from its inception. The California Supreme Court, the Ninth Circuit Federal Court of Appeal and the California courts of appeal have consistently enforced the right of insurers to rescind policies of insurance without requiring the party deceived to present evidence of intentional misrepresentation, intentional concealment of material fact or fraud. All that is required is that the party deceived was in fact deceived about a fact or facts material to the decision to insure. Other states make it more difficult to rescind a policy of insurance and consider states like California to apply the law of rescission in a Draconian fashion.

California rescission statutes do not require that the party deceived prove it was deceived intentionally. All that is required is that the party deceived by a misrepresentation or concealment of a material fact or mistake prove the deception and that the fact misrepresented or concealed was material to the decision to insure or not insure. If deceived the party deceived can return the consideration – the policy or the premium paid – and both parties return to their position immediately before the policy was issued.

Not all states allow rescission for innocent misrepresentations or innocent, inadvertent misrepresentations of material fact or concealment of material fact not related to a loss. They require either fraud or intentional misrepresentation of material fact and some require that the misrepresentation be relevant or related to the pending claim.

"Post Loss Underwriting" is an Oxymoron

Some plaintiffs' lawyers contend that rescission is "post loss underwriting" rather than the exercise of a legitimate equitable remedy as old as the common law. They have gone so far as to convince legislatures to place the term "post loss underwriting" in statutes relating to health insurance plans.

Underwriting, by definition, always occurs before the policy comes into being. Those concerned about rescission should not be concerned about "post loss underwriting" but, rather, should be concerned about the abusive use of the rescission remedy by unscrupulous insurers.

Before one can understand the bases for rescission it is necessary to understand the process called underwriting and how insurers select those people or entities the insurer is willing to insure and determine which persons or entities they are not willing to insure.

Post-claim or post-loss underwriting is the alleged practice of an insurer's failure to engage in adequate underwriting until after a claim is submitted and subsequently denying the claim on the basis that the insured is not entitled to the policy.[8]

What is Insurance Underwriting?

---

[8] . *John Hancock Mut. Life Ins. Co. v. Banerji*, 447 Mass. 875, 858 N.E.2d 277 (2006)

Underwriting is the process of accepting or rejecting risks. It requires a determination of the terms under which the insurance will be written if the risk is acceptable. It is a function unique to the insurance industry. By definition underwriting is a process always performed before a decision is made to insure or not insure and cannot happen after a loss is incurred on the policy.

Modern insurance, when invented in the 18th Century in Lloyd's Coffee Shop on the docks of London, England was a very personal matter. A ship or property owner would discuss with an individual insurer the problems and values which would be involved in a commercial enterprise. They would then agree upon the terms under which the insurer would insure the risk. Together they would draft a contract and the insurer would sign his name at the bottom — he literally underwrote the insurance.

In its original usage, underwriting referred to the operation of the insurance business. In modern usage there is a more restricted meaning applied to the term. Underwriting is a systematic technique for evaluating risks that are offered to an insurer by prospective insureds. The function of underwriting involves evaluating, selecting, classifying, and rating each risk. Underwriting establishes the standards of coverage and amount of protection to be offered to each acceptable risk. It formulates and administers the rules and procedures that are used to ensure that predetermined standards are met by underwriters.

Underwriters are the risk takers, or were hired by the risk takers to act on their behalf. In modern usage in the US underwriting has become more corporate and less individual. Underwriters in the United States are invariably employees of insurance companies and not the actual risk taker who wrote insurance at Lloyd's Coffee Shop. The modern American underwriter performs five basic functions:

1.   Selection of risks;

2.   Classification and rating of the risk;

3.   Policy forms to be used to produce a policy of insurance;

4.   Writing a special manuscript policy to meet the individual needs of a unique insured, and

5.   Retention and reinsurance.

By performing these five functions, the underwriter increases the possibility of securing a safe and profitable distribution of risks so that the insurer can profit from the insurance risks accepted by the underwriter. As one California court stated:

> An insurance company has the *unquestioned right to select those whom it will insure* and to rely upon him who would be insured for such information as it desires as a basis for its determination *to the end that a wise discrimination may be exercised in selecting its risks.*[9] (Emphasis added)

> It is the underwriter who obtains the information necessary to make, and who makes, the decision to select risks the insurer will take. The underwriter expects, based on the information the underwriter receives from the potential insured, that a risk has been agreed that has an opportunity of being profitable. The underwriter, if provided with honest and complete information, is able to wisely discriminate and choose those who can be profitable and refuse those who have a lesser opportunity of being profitable for the insurer.

---

[9] . *Robinson v. Occidental Life Ins. Co.* (1955) 131 Cal.App.2d 581, 586.

The remedy of rescission was created by the ecclesiastical courts of ancient England who were charged with reaching fair results rather than a money judgment to make the plaintiff whole. As courts of equity they voided contracts that were obtained by mistake, misrepresentation, concealment or fraud.

Since the turn of the century the plaintiffs' bar has attempted to defeat the remedy of rescission and allow their clients more access to courts of law assessing damages against insurers and avoid equity courts who, if rescission was established, would have no right to damages at law.

In *Nieto v. Blue Shield of California Life & Health Insurance Co.*[10] the California Court of Appeal dealt with one of the first of the so-called "post-loss underwriting" cases and found that plaintiff Julie Nieto failed to disclose information about her medical condition and treatment on a health insurance application she submitted to Blue Shield of California Life & Health Insurance Company (Blue Shield). The court concluded that the application was a "concealment" as defined by California Insurance Code § 331 and a misrepresentation as defined by California Insurance Code § 359. Based on the material misrepresentation and concealment of material fact Blue Shield rescinded the policy it issued to Nieto.

In response, Nieto filed an action against Blue Shield claiming the rescission was post claim underwriting and an act of bad faith. The trial court granted Blue Shield's motion for summary judgment, ruling that it was entitled to rescission as a matter of law in view of the undisputed evidence that Nieto made material misrepresentations and omissions regarding her medical history.

---

[10] . *Nieto v. Blue Shield of California Life & Health Ins. Co.* (2010) 181 Cal.App.4th 60.

The Court of Appeal affirmed the trial court because it agreed that undisputed evidence established that the information Nieto provided to Blue Shield was false. The court, exercising its decision recognized that the covenant of good faith and fair dealing that applies to all parties to an insurance contract equally allows an insurer to reasonably rely upon the statements made by an applicant on an application for insurance. If the insurer is deceived by the application it has the right to void the contract and put the parties back in the position they were in before the contract was made.

In reaching its conclusion the court noted that in 2005 Blue Shield offered several health insurance plans to individuals. As part of the determination whether to issue coverage, Blue Shield provided an application to each individual seeking coverage that requested detailed information of past and current health problems, treating physicians, prescribed medications and recommended treatment. Using proprietary written guidelines, Blue Shield evaluated the responses provided by each applicant to determine eligibility for health insurance and, if so, at what premium rate.

Blue Shield, like all insurers, relied on the information provided by the applicant when it received the signed application. Blue Shied did not assume the applicant was untruthful nor did it do any investigation to prove she was untruthful at the time it made the decision to insure Nieto. Rather, Blue Shield, believing in and applying the covenant of good faith and fair dealing, only sought to review medical or pharmacy records when the applicant disclosed a condition or treatment that warranted further assessment. When no such condition or treatment was disclosed by the proposed insured, Blue Shield would have no reason to review medical or pharmacy records for the purpose of ascertaining the truthfulness of the applicant's responses.

If the application was incomplete, Blue Shield would contact the applicant to provide additional information. This overall review process is called "underwriting" by the insurance industry.\

Nieto, like applicants for almost every type of insurance policy, signed and dated the application directly below the following attestation:

> "I have read the summary of benefits and the terms and conditions of coverage and authorizations set forth above. I understand and agree to each of them. I alone am responsible for the accuracy and completeness of the information provided on this application. I understand that neither I, nor any family members, will be eligible for coverage if any information is false or incomplete. I also understand that if coverage is issued, it may be cancelled or rescinded upon such a finding."

Nieto confirmed in her deposition that she took responsibility for the accuracy and completeness of the information provided in the application. The trial court expressly rejected Nieto's assertion that Blue Shield had engaged in post loss underwriting in violation of a section of the California Insurance Code explaining that before issuing the policy Blue Shield properly completed its underwriting process and resolved all reasonable questions arising from the information provided by Nieto. It further found the evidence showed that Blue Shield was not required to do more, as there was nothing in the application to alert Blue Shield that Nieto's responses were false. The court reasoned that even if Blue Shield had been required to investigate further, there was no evidence to suggest that it would have learned of Nieto's undisclosed condition and treatment.

The undisputed evidence presented to the court established that Nieto made material misrepresentations and omissions on the application regarding her medical condition and treatment. Nieto responded negatively to the inquiries in the "Medical History" portion of the application, when in fact she had suffered from chronic back problems throughout 2005 and previously. Nieto represented that her last doctor's visit had occurred three years earlier, when in fact she had seen and received significant treatment from two doctors regularly and one at least 17 times between February and May 2005, including the day she signed the application. Finally, Nieto represented that she had not taken or been directed to take any prescription medications in the past year, when in fact she had filled at least 10 prescriptions for four different medications and had received two steroid injections as well as an oral steroid.

The undisputed evidence further established that Nieto's misrepresentations and omissions were material. Even if Blue Shield had not pleaded the issue of its insured's fraud as an affirmative defense, the Court in *Cruey v. Gannett Co.* (1998) 64 Cal.App.4th 356, 367 found that an affirmative defense may be raised for the first time in a summary judgment motion absent a showing of prejudice. Addressing the issue of privilege, the Court stated:

> Given the long-standing California court policy of exercising liberality in permitting amendments to pleadings at any stage of the proceedings [citation] and of disregarding errors or defects in pleadings unless substantial rights are affected [citation], we believe that a party should be permitted to introduce the defense of privilege in a summary judgment procedure so long as the opposing party has adequate notice and opportunity to respond.

Because Nieto had sufficient notice of, and an opportunity to respond to, Blue Shield's motion asserting that her fraud justified rescission of the policy, she suffered no prejudice by responding to the motion on the merits. The trial court determined, as a matter of law, that Blue Shield was entitled to rescind coverage if the undisputed evidence showed that Nieto committed fraud by making material misrepresentations or omissions concerning her medical history or condition to Blue Shield before it issued the policy. Turning to the evidence submitted in connection with the motion, the trial court found "that the undisputed facts established each element of fraud and deceit under California law, with respect to [Nieto's] misrepresentations when applying for coverage with Blue Shield Life."

California law permits an insurer to rescind a policy when the insured has misrepresented or concealed material information in connection with obtaining insurance. (*TIG Ins. Co. of Michigan v. Homestore, Inc.* (2006) 137 Cal.App.4th 749, 755-756.) and *Mitchell v. United National Ins. Co.* (2005) 127 Cal.App.4th 457, 468 (Mitchell), among others. The Insurance Code provides, according to *Mitchell*, a "statutory framework that imposes 'heavy burdens of disclosure' 'upon both parties to a contract of insurance, and any material misrepresentation or the failure, whether intentional or unintentional, to provide requested information permits rescission of the policy by the injured party.' [Citation.]" Discussing the purpose of the statutory scheme, the Court stated:

Requiring full disclosure at the inception of the insurance contract and granting a statutory right to rescind based on concealment or material misrepresentation at that time safeguard the parties' freedom to contract.

Illustrating the application of these provisions, the Court in *Lunardi v. Great-West Life Assurance Co.* (1995) 37 Cal.App.4th 807, affirmed summary judgment in favor of an insurer that rescinded coverage after it discovered the insured had concealed material information about his medical condition during the application process. The insured's obligation to report misstatements in the application is based on the duty of good faith and fair dealing imposed on both parties. The insured's failure to disclose his diagnosis and thereby correct the misstatements in his application constituted a breach of the continuing duty and provided a basis for rescission.

California, by statute and precedent allows courts to confirm rescission of an insurance policy based on an insured's negligent or inadvertent failure to disclose a material fact in the application for insurance.[11]

Nieto relied on the appellate court decision called *Hailey v. California Physicians' Service* (2007) 158 Cal.App.4th 452 (Hailey). She contended, unsuccessfully, that there were triable issues of fact as to whether Blue Shield reasonably completed the medical underwriting process in this case. The Court of Appeal concluded that *Hailey* is both legally and factually inapposite and agreed with the trial court that the undisputed evidence showed that Blue Shield conducted a reasonable investigation and its rescission was not due to any failure to resolve reasonable questions arising from the application. In simple language you cannot lie on an application and then complain that the insurance company did not catch the lies when they were made.

Hailey involved an interpretation of Health and Safety Code section 1389.3, which applies exclusively to health care service plans licensed and regulated by the Department of Managed Health Care. In *Hailey*, the insured completed a Blue Shield application, where Mrs. Hailey claimed she mistakenly believed the application sought information only about her – not her husband and son for whom she also sought coverage; she also claimed that she incorrectly underestimated her husband's weight.

After Blue Shield extended coverage to the insured and her family, the insured's husband was admitted to the hospital for stomach problems and later became completely disabled as the result of an automobile accident. Following the first hospitalization, a Blue Shield investigation revealed that the insured had misrepresented and omitted material information concerning her husband's medical condition.

---

[11] . *Imperial Casualty & Indemnity Co. v. Sogomonian* (1988) 198 Cal.App.3d 169

Blue Shield rescinded the policy. The trial court granted summary judgment in favor of Blue Shield on the insured's complaint for breach of contract and breach of the implied covenant of good faith and fair dealing and on Blue Shield's declaratory relief cross-complaint. The Hailey appellate court reversed, concluding that there were triable issues of fact as to whether Blue Shield engaged in post claims underwriting and whether the insured willfully misrepresented her husband's medical condition.

When the *Hailey* case, on remand, went to trial the Haileys' admitted that they intentionally misrepresented material facts to Blue Shield. Their suit was summarily dismissed mid-trial thereby putting a stake through the heart of the Haileys' post loss underwriting allegation. Blue Shield was required to try the case twice and take it through the litigation and appellate process just to have the Haileys' admit that they obtained the insurance by fraud.

Rescission, as the Court of Appeal found in *Nieto*, has nothing to do with claims.

Underwriting is a decision making process based upon information submitted to the insurer by the proposed insured to convince the insurer to take a risk and insure the proposed insured. When, as did the Haileys and Nieto, the proposed insured lies to obtain the insurance the insurer may seek equity from the court and have the contract voided. To do otherwise would be unfair and allow a fraud to profit from wrongful conduct.

Rescission is an important equitable remedy hoary with age. It should not be limited by claims of bad faith claims handling. Once an insurer learns it was deceived into insuring someone it would not have insured, whether before or after the insurer was sued, it is still entitled to legitimately exercise the right to rescind. It was for that reason that the California Legislature provided both parties to an insurance contract by the California Insurance Code the right to declare a policy void and make both parties whole as if there was never a contract of insurance.

As a general proposition, federal courts sitting in diversity have authority to decide state law claims seeking rescission of an insurance policy.[12]

The California Court of Appeal, the Ninth Circuit Court of Appeal and the California Supreme Court continue to enforce the right and warn those who would attempt to deceive an insurer that they will receive nothing from their deception and find that they may receive no benefit from a legitimate claim that would have been paid if there was no deception.

In *Lewis v. Equity Nat'l Life Ins. Co.*, 637 So.2d 183, 185–86 (Miss.1994) the Mississippi Supreme Court found merit in the plaintiff-insured's claims that the insurer engaged in post-claim underwriting and that the insurer's agent misrepresented information in a policy application. The Court found no evidence of any similar "extreme factual situations" presented by the Plaintiffs in the case. Post-claim underwriting occurs when "an insurer, rather than refusing to write a policy, will wait until after a claim is filed to deny coverage on grounds that the policy should not have been written in the first place." *Dixie Ins. Co. v. Mooneyhan*, 684 So.2d 574, 589 (Miss.1996) (McRae, J., dissenting). The Mississippi Supreme Court has held:

---

[12] . See, e.g., *C.N.R. Atkin v. Smith*, 137 F.3d 1169, 1172 (9th Cir. 1998); *Gasaway v. Nw. Mut. Life Ins. Co.*, 26 F.3d 957, 958 (9th Cir. 1994).

> An insurer has the obligation to its insureds to do its underwriting at the time a policy application is made, not after a claim is filed. It is patently unfair for a claimant to obtain a policy, pay his premiums and operate under the assumption that he is insured against a specified risk, only to learn after he submits a claim that he is not insured, and, therefore, cannot obtain any other policy to cover his loss. The insurer controls when underwriting occurs. It therefore should be estopped from determining whether to accept an insured six months or more after a policy is issued. If the insured is not an acceptable risk, the application should [be] denied up front, not after a policy is issued. This allows the proposed insured to seek other coverage with another company since no company will insure an individual who has suffered serious illness or injury.

As logical as is the analysis of the Mississippi Supreme Court it does not take into consideration the fact that people lie to their insurance companies to obtain insurance. If the lie is not obvious an application revealing an excellent risk may be a total fraud. In such a case the lie is usually never discovered until a claim is made. Post loss underwriting should, in logic, only be applied if the insurer knew the truth at the time the application was submitted and did not exercise the right to refuse the risk. As a result, in *Eagle Transp., LLC v. Scott,* F.Supp.2d, 2012 WL 1712352, (SD Miss., 2012) concluded that since the insurer asked for the information it needed and since the insured provided false answers to the insurer it did not engage in post-claim underwriting and the insured the policy was properly rescinded.

Illinois law has no prohibition on post-claim underwriting. However, while an insurance company might have no duty to conduct an investigation into the truthfulness of an applicant's answer, if it wishes to rescind certain types of policies based on a misrepresentation in the application for that policy, the plain language of Illinois statutes[13] limits the amount of time in which it can do so.

Refusing to apply a post-claim underwriting argument the District Court for the Southern District of West Virginia held that the insurer, MassMutual, put Billy Jordan and Defendant on notice that a material misrepresentation could result in the Policy being rescinded and that there was a two year period after which the policy is incontestable. Further, this notice was provided both when Billy Jordan was applying for the Policy, and in the Policy itself. The insurer was granted summary judgment on its claim of rescission.[14]

In *Harper v. Fidelity and Guar. Life Ins. Co.*, 234 P.3d 1211, 2010 WY 89 (Wyo 2010) the Wyoming Supreme Court rejected claims of post-claim underwriting and affirmed the rescission of an insurance policy because Mr. Harper's application contained omissions and misrepresentations, and summary judgment is appropriate where the misrepresentation is of such a nature that there can be no dispute as to its materiality. Such was the case in this instance. Furthermore, the Wyoming Supreme Court concluded that an insurer is under no duty to investigate the truthfulness of an applicant's responses unless it has notice that those responses might not be truthful or accurate.

---

[13] . *Standard Mut. Ins. Co. v. Jones*, 2012 IL App (4th) 110526, 965 N.E.2d 1129, 358 Ill.Dec. 650

[14] . *Massachusetts Mut. Life Ins. Co. v. Jordan*, Not Reported in F.Supp.2d, 2011 WL 1770435 (S.D.W.Va.)

The Third Circuit Court of Appeal noted that the concept of "post-claim underwriting" itself is nebulous, particularly because it is difficult to draw a distinction between post-claim eligibility investigation and post-claim underwriting. For example, Pennsylvania law provides that it is not bad faith to conduct a thorough investigation into a questionable claim. The insured's concept of "post-claim underwriting" would usurp this general principal and prevent insurers from engaging in post-claim investigations, even in the face of incontrovertible evidence that an insured made a clear misrepresentation.[15] The Third Circuit, so finding, recognized that claims of post-claim underwriting as a method of preventing an insurer from rescinding a policy, was an invitation to fraud and deprived the insurer of the fairness essential to a claim of rescission.

In *Hornback v. Bankers Life Ins. Co.*, 176 S.W.3d 699 Ky App, 2005, the Kentucky court of appeal concluded that an insurance company that issues a policy based on the applicant's answers, without any investigation, is not precluded from raising the defense of fraud or material misrepresentation after a claim is submitted. (*State Farm Mut. Auto. Ins. Co. v. Crouch*, 706 S.W.2d 203, 206 (Ky.App.1986)). When an insured misrepresents material facts on the application, the insurer is justified in denying coverage and rescinding the policy immediately upon discovering that it had been deceived. In so finding the Court of Appeal refused to consider claims of post-claim underwriting and affirmed the rescission.

---

[15] . *Northwestern Mut. Life Ins. Co. v. Babayan*, 430 F.3d 121 (CA 3 (PA) 2005)

Claims of post-claim or post-loss underwriting should be looked at with a great deal of skepticism. As the *Hailey* case made clear even when rescission was refused and the case was sent back to the trial court for trial, the Hailey's, on cross-examination, admitted that they intentionally misrepresented their health conditions when applying for the insurance. Their suit was immediately dismissed for fraud in the inception and they were lucky that they were not prosecuted for attempted insurance fraud. They clearly cost their putative insurer a great deal of money defending through trial, an appeal and a second trial, only to admit fraud. They hoped, by claiming the tort of bad faith, to bludgeon the insurer into a settlement for fear of a bad faith judgment with punitive and tort damages available in addition to the benefits promised by the policy.

The theory of post-claim underwriting sounds fair, on its face, sufficient to cause some states to enact legislation prohibiting it. Once the theory is taken to its logical ending it is really a method to assist unscrupulous insureds to defraud their insurer. For example if proposed insured, suffering from Ebola, applies for insurance and claims perfect health, and received a life insurance policy based on the application, should not be able to claim that the insurer when it rescinds the policy after the Ebola victims death, to be refused rescission because it is applying post-claim underwriting. What it is actually doing is seeking fairness from a court to prevent it from honoring a fraud

Rescission Without Sufficient Evidence is Dangerous

Although it appears to be relatively easy to rescind a policy of insurance in California. If evidence is available to prove misrepresentation, concealment or mistake of a fact material to the decision to insure or not insure, rescission will only be enforced because equity requires fairness. California, by statute, recognizes that it would not be fair to require an insurer to insure a person who had deceived it about the risk it was being asked to take. California also believes it would be unfair for an insured to be bound by a policy of insurance about whose provisions the insured was deceived. The decision to rescind must be tempered by the warning from the court of appeal that:

> "Our conclusion here should not result in an assumption by insurers that policy liability can, with impunity, be avoided or delayed by assertion of a claim for rescission. *That is a tactic which is fraught with peril.* Where no valid ground for rescission exists, the threat or attempt to seek such relief may itself constitute (1) a breach of the covenant of good faith and fair dealing which is implied in the policy (*Fletcher v. Western National Life Ins. Co.* (1970) 10 Cal. App. 3d 376, 392, 401 [89 Cal. Rptr. 78, 47 A.L.R.3d 286]) and/or (2) the commission of one or more of the unfair claims settlement practices proscribed by Insurance Code section 790.03, subdivision (h)."[16] (Emphasis added.)

---

[16] . *Imperial Casualty & Indemnity Co. v. Sogomonian* (1988) 198 Cal.App.3d 169

Whenever an insurer or an insured attempts to rescind a policy of insurance it must have conducted a complete and thorough investigation into the acquisition of the policy, the representations made by all parties before the policy was acquired, interviewed the agents, brokers and insureds to determine representations made and intent of the parties. Then, after the investigation is completed the party seeking rescission must seek the advice and counsel of an experienced coverage lawyer.

Depending on the facts and the advice of counsel rescission can be completed by letter or the filing of a suit seeking declaratory relief from a court of competent jurisdiction affirming the opinion that the contract should be rescinded and the parties placed in the same status as they were before the contract was first made

0In England, before there was a United States of America, courts were divided between law courts that dealt with money damages and courts of equity that existed only to allow for dealing fairly with litigants. Rescission was one of those ancient equitable remedies where two contracting parties sought to avoid a contract because there was a mistake as to the reason for the contract, misrepresentation, concealment or fraud. The court would order the contract void *ab initio,* that is, from its inception with each party returning the consideration received for the contract. When dealing with an insurance contract, if the court found rescission was appropriate, the contract was declared void, the insurer was required to return the premium to the insured and the insured was required to return the contract to the insurer and both would treat the insurance contract as if it never existed.

One of the first, if not the first insurance rescission case which also reported that insurance was a contract of utmost good faith, was decided by Lord Mansfield in the British House of Lords, in 1776. Since it is a first and uses some ancient English usages and spellings, it is worthy of being read in full and in its original language.

In *Illinois, Certain Underwriters at Lloyd's, London v. Abbott Laboratories*, 2014 IL App (1st) 132020, 16 N.E.3d 747, 384 Ill.Dec. 354 the Illinois Court of Appeal concluded that an insurer seeking to rescind an insurance contract based upon fraud or misrepresentation must choose to do so promptly after learning of the alleged fraud or misrepresentation; by not taking such necessary steps to set aside a claimed fraudulent agreement in a timely manner, a party may be found to have ratified it and be barred from later attempting to rescind it. The time limit to rescind is a "reasonable" amount of time. What is "reasonable" is subjective and difficult to pin down. The prudent insurer will, immediately upon learning of facts sufficient to establish that rescission is appropriate, will notify the insured of the rescission and either offer to or actually return the premium. Delay, if any, should be limited to the time needed to obtain the advice and counsel of competent insurance coverage counsel.

In Michigan, an insured's representation in her oral application for homeowner's insurance, that her property taxes were not delinquent for two or more years, was material and the insurer relied on it. As required under Michigan law for an insurer to rescind the policy if the representation was false the insurer declared it would not have issued the policy had it known that the taxes were two years or more delinquent at the time of the application. The basis of the rescission was a Michigan statute that precluded eligibility for homeowner's insurance if real property taxes for the dwelling were delinquent for two or more years.[17]

---

[17] . *Hatcher v. Nationwide Property & Cas. Ins. Co.*, --- F.Supp.2d ----, 2014 WL 3700619 (E.D.Mich., 2014)

A party "may consent to rescission by the other party either impliedly or by conduct."[18] In *McCollum*, the Court found that an insurance customer's conduct in demanding and accepting the return of a previously tendered premium for certain coverage manifested an intent to rescind the contract for that coverage, even though there was no explicit agreement to rescind.[19]

In New York, to establish the right to rescind an insurance policy, an insurer must show that its insured made a material misrepresentation of fact when he or she secured the policy.[20] A misrepresentation is material if the insurer would not have issued the policy had it known the facts misrepresented. To establish materiality as a matter of law, the insurer must present documentation concerning its underwriting practices, such as underwriting manuals, bulletins, or rules pertaining to similar risks, that show that it would not have issued the same policy if the correct information had been disclosed in the application.[21]

In New Jersey, knowledge of the statement's falsity is not a prerequisite for rescission of an insurance policy unless the applicant made the statement in response to a subjective question e.g. a question asking what the applicant believes or is aware of.[22]

---

[18] . *Nationwide Mut. Ins. Co. v. McCollum*, 179 Ga.App. 500, 502(1), 347 S.E.2d 231 (1986)

[19] . *Thompson v. Lovett*, 328 Ga.App. 573, 760 S.E.2d 246 (2014); see appendix for a form of agreement to mutually rescind a policy of insurance.

[20] . *Interboro Ins. Co. v. Fatmir*, 89 A.D.3d 993, 993–994, 933 N.Y.S.2d 343; *Meah v. A. Aleem Constr., Inc.*, 105 A.D.3d 1017, 1019, 963 N.Y.S.2d 714).

[21] . *Lema v. Tower Ins. Co. of New York*, 119 A.D.3d 657, 990 N.Y.S.2d 231, 2014 N.Y. Slip Op. 05162

Material misrepresentations in an application for an insurance policy may, and usually will, prevent recovery on the policy.[23] A representation in an application for an insurance policy is deemed material if the knowledge or ignorance of it would naturally influence the judgment of the insurer in making the contract. In an application for a life insurance policy, written questions and answers relating to health are deemed material as a matter of law.[24]

Answers made in response to questions in the application as to prior illness, consultation with physicians and applications for other insurance, where the applicant declares that they are true and offers them as an inducement to the issuance of the policy, are deemed material as a matter of law. It is well settled that a misrepresentation of a material fact, or the suppression thereof, in an application for insurance, will avoid the policy even though the assured be innocent of fraud or an intention to deceive or to wrongfully induce the insurer to act, or whether the statement was made in ignorance or good faith, or unintentionally.[25]

To establish the right to rescind an insurance policy in New York, an insurer must demonstrate that the insured made a material misrepresentation. A misrepresentation is material if the insurer would not have issued the policy had it known the facts misrepresented.[26]

---

[22] . *Ledley v. William Penn Life Ins. Co.,* 651 A.2d 92 (N.J.1995)); *Colony Ins. Co. v. Kwasnik, Kanowitz & Associates, P.C.,* Slip Copy, 2014 WL 2920810 (D.N.J.)

[23] . *Luther v. Seawell,* 191 N.C.App. 139, 662 S.E.2d 1, 4 (N.C.App.2008) (citing N.C. Gen.Stat. § 58–3–10).

[24] . *Ward v. Durham Life Ins. Co.,* 325 N.C. 202, 381 S.E.2d 698, 702 (N.C.1989); see also *Fountain & Herrington, Inc. v. Mut. Life Ins. Co. of N.Y.,* 55 F.2d 120, 123 (4th Cir.1932)

[25] . *Reliastar Life Ins. Co. v. Laschkewitsch,* Slip Copy, 2014 WL 2211033 (E.D.N.C., 2014)

In Kentucky, when the plaintiff failed to dispute that the alleged misrepresentations were material in her response brief to the motion for summary judgment, she cannot seek to alter the judgment based on Defendant's failure to establish that there is no genuine dispute regarding materiality. Proof of misrepresentation and materiality is sufficient to support a rescission.[27]

Automobile insurance policies, like other policies, are subject to rescission. Since auto policies are ubiquitous, there is a volume of cases involving attempts to rescind policies of automobile liability and comprehensive and collision insurance. Once the contract is made, if made without misrepresentation or concealment of material fact, the policy will be enforced. If, however, the insured misrepresents material facts before the policy was agreed to and deceives the insurer about a material fact then the policy may be rescinded from its inception.

---

[26] . *Zilkha v. Mutual Life Ins. Co. of N.Y.*, 287 A.D.2d 713, 714, 732 N.Y.S.2d 51; see Insurance Law § 3105[b]; *Parmar v. Hermitage Ins. Co.*, 21 A.D.3d 538, 540, 800 N.Y.S.2d 726). Whether a misrepresentation is material is generally a question of fact for the jury (see *Schirmer v. Penkert*, 41 A.D.3d 688, 690, 840 N.Y.S.2d 796; *Process Plants Corp. v. Beneficial Natl. Life Ins. Co.*, 53 A.D.2d 214, 216, 385 N.Y.S.2d 308, affd. 42 N.Y.2d 928, 397 N.Y.S.2d 1007, 366 N.E.2d 1361).

[27] . *Koch v. Owners Ins. Co.*, 996 F.Supp.2d 531 (2014)

The Pennsylvania Supreme Court has held that an automobile insurance policy cannot be retroactively rescinded with respect to third parties who were harmed through no fault of their own. During his examination before trial, plaintiff's assignor testified that his mother, the insured, had never resided in Allentown, Pennsylvania, and that he had driven his mother to Pennsylvania for the sole purpose of renewing her automobile insurance because the insurance was cheaper in Pennsylvania than in New York. Inasmuch as the aforementioned acts of the assignor make him complicit in the fraud perpetrated by his mother, he is not an innocent third party and, therefore, rescission of the subject insurance policy is effective with respect to him.[28]

The Pennsylvania Supreme Court has held, however, that while an automobile insurance policy may be retroactively rescinded as to an insured who has made a misrepresentation material to the acceptance of risk by the insurer, the policy may not be retroactively rescinded with respect to third parties "who are innocent of trickery, and injured through no fault of their own. Although defendant, in its motion papers, set forth facts tending to demonstrate that the insured was the actual perpetrator of a fraud, and that, based on that fact, it rescinded the policy in accordance with Pennsylvania law, defendant's submissions did not conclusively establish that plaintiff's assignor was not an innocent third party.[29]

---

[28] . Optimal Well–Being Chiropractic, P.C. v. Infinity Ins. Co., --- N.Y.S.2d ----, 2014 WL 4065047 (N.Y.Sup.App.Term), 2014 N.Y. Slip Op. 24227; for additional information re public policy and rescission see chapter 7 below.

[29] . *Erie Ins. Exch. v. Lake*, 543 Pa 363, 375, 671 A.2d 681, 687 [1996]; *Delta Diagnostic Radiology, P.C. v. Infinity Group*, 43 Misc.3d 130(A), 988 N.Y.S.2d 522 (Table), 2014 WL 1508497 (N.Y.Sup.App.Term), 2014 N.Y. Slip Op. 50602

In the field of automobile insurance, New Jersey courts have held that the rescission remedy available to insurance carriers when a policy was procured by means of a material misrepresentation may not infringe upon the rights of innocent third parties who might need to rely on insurance coverage to compensate them for their injuries.[30] New Jersey courts distinguish between the wrongdoing insured, who procured the policy fraudulently or otherwise failed to comply with the terms of the policy, and an innocent third party, who had nothing to do with the fraud or breach of the policy.[31]

In *Civil Service Employees Insurance Co. v. Blake,* 245 Cal. App. 2d 196, 53 Cal. Rptr. 701(Cal.App.Dist.2 09/26/1966) the California Court of Appeal was faced with a claim by the insurer seeking a declaration that the policy is void because of fraudulent statements in defendant's application for the policy.

---

[30] . *Rutgers Cas. Ins. Co. v. LaCroix,* 194 N.J . 515, 524–31, 946 A.2d 1027 (2008); *Fisher v. N.J. Auto. Full Ins. Underwriting Ass'n*, 224 N.J.Super. 552, 557–59, 540 A.2d 1344 (App.Div.1988).

[31] . *Csap v. American Millennium Ins. Co.,* Not Reported in A.3d, 2014 WL 2011714 (N.J.Super.A.D. 2014)

The first question on the application was "Have you or any other driver of this car: (A) Any chronic ailment? (espec. Heart disease, Epilepsy, Fainting spells, etc.)" Blake answered "Yes. In 1950 but none after." In fact, Blake had had epileptic blackouts continuously from 1949 to at least 1960. In 1949 Blake had had a blackout while driving and caused an accident in which three persons had been killed. The second question was "Have you or any other driver of this car: (C) Ever had your driver's license revoked, suspended, or restricted?" Blake answered "No" although in fact his license had been surrendered in 1950 and revoked in 1959 and his other applications for a license had been denied. The evidence showed that Blake intentionally answered these two questions falsely, that Tucker, the agent who took Blake's application, had no knowledge of his physical condition or his driving history, that the insurance company would not have issued the policy had the questions in the application been answered truthfully.

During the period covered by the policy Blake had an automobile accident involving Carter, and Carter sued Blake for personal injuries. Thereafter the company discovered Blake's true health history and rescinded its policy. However, Blake and Carter contend the insurance company was not, as a matter of law, entitled to rely on the false representations in Blake's application for insurance in 1962, because in 1957 it had issued a policy of insurance to Blake through an agent of the company named Reinhart, and at that time Reinhart had known that Blake was subject to blackouts and was not licensed to drive.

Blake and Carter argue the general rule that a principal is charged with knowledge of all material facts known to its agent. They contend that Reinhart's uncommunicated knowledge in 1957 of Blake's health and driving record was imputed to the company in 1962 when a new application for insurance was submitted by Blake through a different agent; that therefore, the company could not have relied on the false representations in the 1962 application, because knowledge of their falsity was legally imputed to the company.

The court concluded that the company was justified in proceeding with cancellation by routine and ordered business practices rather than by way of a crash program. The court found no undue delay in the company's action in following up available leads on the subject of false representations, nor any undue delay in the company's notice of rescission once it had discovered false representations about health.

Sometimes the misrepresentation that is the basis for a claim of rescission is so obvious the court will have no problem affirming the rescission. Even though a third person was injured by the insured before the policy was rescinded there was no recovery for the insured or the injured party because of the egregious nature of the misrepresentation.

New York Vehicle and Traffic Law provides that "[n]o contract of insurance for which a certificate of insurance has been filed with the commissioner shall be terminated by cancellation by the insurer until at least twenty days after mailing to the named insured at the address shown on the policy." N.Y.Veh. & Traf. L. § 313.1(a). "New York courts hold this provision to prohibit rescission of auto insurance policies ab initio, even when the policyholder made fraudulent misrepresentations of material issues in obtaining the policy." *Am. Centennial Ins. Co. v. Sinkler*, 903 F.Supp. 408, 410–11 (E.D.N.Y.1995) (Weinstein, J.). Put another way, New York courts have read its laws establishing compulsory automobile insurance as eliminating insurers' common law right of rescission for fraud or misrepresentation, with the minor exception of notice pursuant to statute.[32]

Although Connecticut law provides for a common law right to retroactively rescind an automobile insurance policy, in the case of *Munroe v. Great American Ins. Co.* (234 Conn 182, 193, 661 A.2d 581 [1995]), the Connecticut Supreme Court held that the Connecticut Legislature did not intend that an insurer's common law right of rescission as to innocent third-party victims, such as involved herein, survive the enactment of the Connecticut automobile insurance statutes. Therefore, any retroactive rescission of the subject insurance policy did not affect the rights of the innocent third-party assignors, and defendant's cross motion for summary judgment dismissing the complaint on the ground of lack on coverage due to the retroactive rescission of the automobile insurance policy was properly denied. Accordingly, as defendant raises no issue with respect to plaintiff's prima facie showing upon its motion for summary judgment, the order is affirmed.[33]

---

[32] . American Service Ins. Co. v. Garcia, Not Reported in F.Supp.2d, 2013 WL 865878 (S.D.N.Y., 2013)

[33] . *W.H.O. Acupuncture, P.C. v. Infinity Ins. Co.*, 37 Misc.3d 130(A), 961 N.Y.S.2d 362 (Table),

Similarly, the statutory right to rescind granted by Fla. Stat. § 627.409 does not apply to certain specifically identified types of insurance. [See Fla. Stat. § 627.401.] The excluded types of insurance do not include automobile insurance in general, or automobile insurance where an innocent third-party has been injured and has filed a claim before the rescission of the policy. Absent an express exclusion by the Florida legislature, the statutory right to rescission applies to automobile insurance policies. *United Auto. Ins. Co. v. Salgado*, 22 So.3d 594 (Fla. 3d DCA 2009) held that "absent an express exclusion by the legislature, the right of rescission contained in section 627.409, Florida Statutes (2003), applies to PIP insurance contracts issued pursuant to the Florida Motor Vehicle No–Fault Law." Additionally, Florida courts have already found that the statutory right to rescission applies in a situation such as in this case. E.g., *Redland Ins. Co. v. Cem Site Constructors, Inc.* 86 So.3d 1259 (Fla. 2d DCA 2012); *Mercury Ins. Co. of Fla. v. Markham*, 36 So.3d 730 (Fla. 1st DCA 2010); *Penaranda v. Progressive Am. Ins. Co.*, 747 So.2d 953 (Fla. 2d DCA 1999). Regardless, depending on the facts of the case the right to rescission can be available. The insurer had no affirmative obligation to conduct an investigation of the driving history before issuing an insurance policy. Since the court found that the misrepresentations by the insured were intentional it did not matter because even an unintentional misrepresentation would support rescission, *Carter v. United of Omaha Life Ins.*, 685 So.2d 2, 6 (Fla. 1st DCA 1996) that held: "Since the statute does not contain a knowledge or intent element, even unintentional or unknowing misstatements may prevent recovery under a policy, if such statements alter the risk or the likelihood of coverage."[34]   In *Standard Accident*

2012 WL 5049033 (N.Y.Sup.App.Term), 2012 N.Y. Slip Op. 51965(U).

[34] . *State Farm Mut. Auto. Ins. Co. v. Cockram,* Not

Insurance Co. v. Pratt, 130 Cal. App. 2d 151, 278 P.2d 489 (Cal.App.Dist.4 01/07/1955) the application was accepted by the Interinsurance Exchange of the Automobile Club of Southern California and the policy of insurance was issued by the plaintiff Standard Accident Insurance Company on June 12, 1951. The policy contains no reference to the application or to the representations made therein by Pratt. Attached to the face of the policy is a statement designated "Declarations," which likewise contains no reference to the application and relates to matters which are not in dispute. There is a conflict in the evidence as to whether Pratt had any "physical impairments" as those words are used in the policy and understood by the parties. The trial court found in this connection that "David S. Pratt had a physical impairment, to wit, faulty vision, and at all times herein mentioned had faulty vision, a condition known to him at the time he made said application for automobile liability insurance contract." This finding is supported by substantial evidence and cannot be disturbed on appeal. (*Berniker v. Berniker,* 30 Cal. 2d 439, 444 [182 P.2d 557].) The trial court further found that at the time he made application for said automobile insurance contract defendant David S. Pratt "Did not have nor possess a valid California operator's license nor has he ever had or ever possessed, at any time mentioned herein, a valid California operator's license." This finding is also supported by substantial evidence and is not here questioned.

Reported in F.Supp.2d, 2012 WL 4903271 (M.D.Fla.), 23 Fla. L. Weekly Fed. D 371 (2012)

Section 359 of the California Insurance Code provides that "If a representation is false in a material point, whether affirmative or promissory, the injured party is entitled to rescind the contract from the time the representation became false. Section 351 of said code provides that "A representation may be made at the time of, or before, the issuance of the policy. Section 331 of said code provides that "Concealment, whether intentional or unintentional, entitles the injured party to rescind insurance.

Subrogation and the Tort Remedy

When an insurer pays a claim resulting from the conduct of a third person it obtains a right of subrogation to recover from the wrongdoer the amounts paid as if it was the person it insured.

i. Negligence

When one person does a wrong to another it is called a "tort." Negligence is a type of tort. A tort can be either accidental or intentional. In either event the person to whom the wrong is done is able to sue for the damages he or she suffers as a result of that wrong. An insurer can step in the shoes of the insured and file the same suit if it paid the insured for the same damages. To establish a cause of action in negligence the subrogating insurer must prove:

- the wrongdoer had a duty not to harm the property of the insured;
- he or she breached that duty;
- as a proximate result of the breach the property of the insured was damaged; and
- the insurer paid the insured for the damages incurred.[15]

The presumption of negligence (sometimes called "negligence per se") arises if (1) the defendant violated a statute; (2) the violation proximately caused the plaintiff's injury; (3) the injury resulted from the kind of occurrence the statute was designed to prevent; and (4) the plaintiff was one of the class of persons the statute was intended to protect.[16]

When the law of negligence was young the contributory negligence of the victim of an accident was an absolute defense to a negligence suit. A person who was only 1% responsible for an accident could recover nothing from the person 99% responsible for the loss. The courts found such results to be unfair. The comparative negligence doctrine was established to cure the draconian nature of the contributory negligence defense. It makes almost every loss recoverable, at least in part, since most accidents that cause damage to property are the result of the partially negligent acts of more than one person. In essence, the comparative negligence doctrine holds that if a plaintiff contributes, in part, to his injury by his own negligence his recovery against the other party is reduced by the percentage of his negligence. A subrogating insurer should recognize that recovery of a part of a loss is better than no recovery at all.

Comparative negligence means a failure to do an act that a reasonably careful person would do, or the doing of an act that a reasonably careful person would not do, under the same or similar circumstances, to protect oneself from bodily injury.[LYONS, 770 P.2d At 1254; BURR V. GREEN BROS. SHEET METAL, INC., 159 Colo. 25, 35–36, 409 P.2d 511, 516–17 (1966).]A defendant may not raise a defense of comparative negligence as a matter of law if, under the circumstances, the plaintiff "did all he was legally required to do," and had no duty to do more. RINGSBY TRUCK LINES, INC. V. BRADFIELD, 193 Colo. 151, 563 P.2d 939, 942 (1977) holding that where defendant was driving toward plaintiff in the wrong lane, plaintiff who slowed and pulled over was "not required to drive his vehicle into the ditch" and thus comparative negligence was properly withdrawn from the jury's consideration. [*P.W. v. Children's Hospital* Colorado, Supreme Court of Colorado, 364 P.3d 891, 2016 CO 6 (2016)]

ii. Strict Liability

To establish a cause of action for strict liability in tort, the subrogating insurer must, with evidence gathered by the adjuster, prove the following:

- that there is a product (a manufactured thing);
- that there is a defect in the product;
- that damage has been done to the property of a third person, the insured; and
- that the defect in the product was the proximate or legal cause of the damage.

A defendant who performs an abnormally dangerous or ultrahazardous activity will be subject to liability for damages resulting from that activity, even if the defendant has exercised the utmost care to prevent the harm. This doctrine for imposing strict liability originated in the English case *Rylands v. Fletcher*, (1868) UKHL 1, 3 L.R. (H.L.) 330. Liability for an abnormally dangerous or ultrahazardous activity is considered strict "because the defendant's negligence or lack thereof is irrelevant. Rather, the liability arises out of the abnormal danger of the activity itself, and the risk that it creates, of harm to those in the vicinity. It is based on a policy of the law that imposes upon anyone, who for her own purposes creates an abnormal risk of harm to her neighbors, the responsibility of relieving against that harm when it does in fact occur." [*Great American Ins. Co. v. Heneghan Wrecking and Excavating*, Appellate Court of Illinois, 2015 IL App (1st) 133376, 46 N.E.3d 859, 399 Ill.Dec. 540 (2015)]

Strict liability in tort makes proof somewhat simpler than negligence (since there is no need to prove duty or breach of the duty) but is not absolute liability. The doctrine of comparative fault applies in strict liability as it does in negligence cases.

iii. The Contract Remedy

A contract is an agreement, either oral or written, where one person, for some consideration (like money, property, or a promise to do or not do some act) agrees to do (or not do) something. If the contract is broken, or breached, then the person who was entitled to receive some service or thing is entitled to recover in a court of law the damages he or she incurred as a result of the breach. If an insurer pays the damages, it may step in the shoes of the insured and sue for the breach.

The elements of breach of contract are: (1) the contract, (2) plaintiff's performance or excuse for nonperformance, (3) defendant's breach, and (4) the resulting damages to plaintiff. [*Kumaraperu v. Feldsted*, 237 Cal.App.4th 60, 187 Cal.Rptr. 3d 583 (2015)] If an insurer can meet all four elements it can prove its subrogation rights and obtain judgment from the person breaching the contract.

iv. The Equitable Remedy

Equity allows creative remedies for wrongs that do not fit within the confines of traditional tort or contract remedies (*i.e.*, with cash). The ancient maxim "for every wrong there is a remedy" (California Civil Code § 3523) applies to subrogation rights. The maxims were adopted from the common law of England and are relied on in all jurisdictions. In California, the maxims were codified in its Civil Code.

In *Westchester Fire Insurance Company v. Admiral Insurance Company*, No. 2-01-227-Cv (Tex. App.Dist.2 06/26/2003), the Texas Court of Appeal stated the elements of a right to equitable remedy as:

"[T]he two key elements of equitable subrogation are 1) that the party on whose behalf the claimant discharged a debt was primarily liable on the debt, and 2) that the claimant paid the debt involuntarily." … In this case, Admiral did not contend that Westchester was a volunteer, but that Admiral did not owe a debt to its insured for the punitive damages, treble damages, and attorney's fees because they were not covered under Admiral's policy.

The purpose of equitable subrogation is "to prevent forfeiture and unjust enrichment." [Eastern Savings Bank, FSB v. Pappas, 829 A.2d 953, 957 (D.C.2003)]

Equitable subrogation is a doctrine that allows one who has discharged the debt of another to succeed to the rights of the satisfied creditor. For example, if Creditor # 3 pays off a debt owed to Creditor # 1 by the same debtor, equitable subrogation would enable Creditor # 3 to jump ahead of Creditor # 2 in priority for repayment. The doctrine, which began in the English courts of equity as a way for a surety to seek repayment from a defaulting debtor, has been applied by the Delaware Court of Chancery for over a century. [*Eastern Savings Bank, FSB v. Cach*, LLC, Supreme Court of Delaware, 124 A.3d 585 (2015)]

Specific performance is an equitable remedy which compels someone to do what he or she has promised to do, such as a turn over possession of property.

The Fire Case as a Basis for Subrogation

Fires do not normally occur absent the negligence of some person. The adjuster must determine how the fire started, where the fire started, and why it spread.

Hiring a fire cause investigator is a good investment in every fire case. If the insured did not accidentally or intentionally set the fire then the adjuster should be able to exercise the right to subrogation recovery.

If an insured clumsily tips over a candle and ignites his sofa you might think there was no subrogation possible. However, the adjuster must determine:

- Who designed and manufactured the candle? Was it safe for the clumsy insured to use?
- Who designed and manufactured the sofa? Was it too easy to burn and thus unsafe?
- Who placed the candle where the insured could knock it over? Did he or she breach a duty of care that would cause the insured to foresee a fire?

The Auto Accident Case as a Basis For Subrogation

The insured admits he ran a red light and hit a third party. Even this fact situation has a possibility of subrogation. Suppose there was an overhanging tree that had obscured the insured's vision and he could not see the light. The insured, and his insurer, may have a right back against the owner of the tree, or possibly the city, for maintaining its property in a dangerous condition: the stop lights were hidden from the view of motorists.

Leases as a Basis for Subrogation

Almost every lease of real or personal property imposes obligations on the lessee and provides rights to the lessor. An insurer may, under the right to subrogation, exercise the rights provided by a lease agreement. Therefore, a thorough claims investigation must include this agreement in every loss where the property is rented by or to an insured.

The lease usually tells, as between the lessor and the lessee, who is responsible for any casualty to particular pieces of property. The adjuster may find that another insurer, that of the lessor, also insures the tenants' improvements and betterments and is responsible under the lease for the cost to repair them. The lease may contain an express or implied waiver of subrogation. The adjuster must obtain all of the following:

- the full name of the insured and his capacity (an individual, corporate officer, employee, trustee or partner);
- the date, place, and facts of the loss;
- if a product is involved, the identity of the product including its name, manufacturer, model number, serial number and distributor;
- the remains of any potentially defective product, secured by an independent testing laboratory;
- photographs of everything;
- copies of all relevant contracts and policies of insurance;
- the names and addresses of all witnesses and any people involved with the origin of the loss even if they are not witnesses; and
- a recorded or signed statement from the insured and all witnesses.

The adjuster must carefully document all damages and secure the services of an expert, if a product is involved, or the cause of loss warrants.

After completing the investigation, the adjuster must report his or her conclusion as to the party or parties at fault. Since it will almost never be only one person or entity, the adjuster should estimate the percentages of fault attributable to each party. The adjuster must get a sworn proof of loss properly notarized or signed under penalty of perjury by the insured. The adjuster must have the insured sign a subrogation agreement that assigns to the company all of the rights of the insured.

If the adjuster cannot resolve the subrogation claim short of litigation the information gathered should be given to a lawyer so that he or she may adequately pursue the right of the insurer to subrogation in the courts.

For the subrogation effort to be successful, the adjuster should hire his or her own expert for the case. If the adjuster joins with another adjuster representing a different party to hire an expert some courts will conclude that the insurer has waived the work product protection and require that the reports be disclosed to all defendants. Sometimes the reports of the original expert are less than adequate and can be kept from the defendants by exercise of the work product protection. If the adjuster shares the expert with other insurers the adjuster may compel the lawyer to disclose information that, because it was written early in the investigation, may be wrong and/or unfavorable to the insurer's cause.

The adjuster should not let the expert write a report unless it is totally favorable to the case. If the report is unfavorable, the expert should be advised not to write a report. The expert can then be declared to be a consultant and cannot, as a result, be hired by the other side. His or her opinions will be protected work product that cannot be discovered. The expert may have made a mistake, and this would give the insurer the opportunity to get a more competent expert. There is no duty of good faith to tortfeasors. The insured, if he was not insured, would have no obligation to tell a third party responsible for his injury that he had a poorly written expert report that helps the other side.

The adjuster should not attempt to handle a cause investigation that is beyond his or her experience. If the loss is suspicious or requires special expertise, the adjuster should hire an expert. The expert can then give opinions in court, if necessary, to establish the subrogation right of the insurer. The adjuster must never assume anything that cannot be proven.

The adjuster must preserve the evidence before letting the salvage be carted away. The salvage remaining after a loss can be extremely valuable in establishing the cause and extent of loss. That portion of the salvage that relates to the cause of loss should be preserved carefully so that it is available to prove the insurer's case in court. Allowing such evidence to be disposed of after a loss can give rise to a suit for spoliation of evidence that could expose the insured and the insurer to claims for damages.

The adjuster should speak with the official investigators. The opinions of official investigators, like an arson investigator, may provide an unbiased expert opinion that will carry more weight with a lay jury than an expert who is paid a fee for his or her opinions. The opinions of the official investigators also provide a means to weigh and evaluate the opinions of private experts.

The adjuster should not let the insured release the liability of anyone who may be responsible for the damage to the property that is the subject of the insurance.. The adjuster can explain to the insured that once the claim is paid, the insurer has the right to subrogation, and if the insured deprives the insurer of its right of subrogation the insured can find itself with no coverage at all. If the insured signs a release after the loss, the insurer— whose subrogation rights are derivative only—can lose the right of subrogation. In California, the Court of Appeal in *Liberty Mutual Insurance Co. v. Altfillisch Construction Co.*, 70 Cal.App.3d 789, 139 Cal. Rptr. 91 (Cal. App. Dist. 4 06/16/1977), held that an insured was required to return to the insurer the money paid because it released the responsible party without permission and deprived the insurer of its right of subrogation.

The U.S. Court of Appeal for the Sixth Circuit came to a similar result as the California Court of Appeal in *Liberty Mutual*[17] concluding that because it entered into a general release with the party who damaged the property insured by Westfield, and hence impaired Westfield's right of subrogation in breach of the parties' policy for property insurance. The court, in reaching its decision, relied on cases from other jurisdictions.[18] *Stolaruk* held that an insured is barred from recovery under an insurance policy if it extinguishes the insurer's right of subrogation by releasing a tortfeasor. In addition, the Michigan Court of Appeal and an encyclopedia held: "As a general rule, an insured who deprives an insurer, by settlement and release, of its right of subrogation against a wrongdoer, thereby provides the insurer with a complete defense to an action on the policy."[19]

Some policies of first party property insurance allow an insured to waive the right of subrogation before the loss to anyone. Some policies allow the insured to waive the right of its insurer to subrogation after the loss to certain classes of individuals like tenants. If the insured waives subrogation within the rights provided by the policy, the insurer can close its file—it has given away all rights to subrogation and cannot succeed.

A Vermont court found that (1) waiver-of-subrogation provision in construction contract did not violate public policy despite allegation of gross negligence; (2) waiver-of-subrogation provision could be enforced even though general contractor failed to obtain waivers from subcontractors; and (3) waiver-of-subrogation provision was applicable to costs stemming from services that were specifically excluded from construction contract. [*Behr v. Hook*, Supreme Court of Vermont, 173 Vt.122, 787 A.2d 499 (2001)]

In cases involving waivers of subrogation there is no risk that an injured party will be left uncompensated, and it is irrelevant to the injured party whether it is compensated by the grossly negligent party or an insurer. [*Reliance National v. Knowles Industrial Services, Corp*, Supreme Judicial Court of Maine, 868 A.2d 220, 2005 ME 29 (2005)]

Preparing a Case for Trial

Selecting and Working with Counsel

Retaining an Attorney

In instances where insurance claims may entail litigation, insurers must move quickly to engage counsel. When an attorney is retained to defend a person insured, the fact should be documented in writing by the attorney, the adjuster, and the insured who is to be defended. If the attorney is being retained for the first time by the insurer, the insurer should obtain an engagement letter from the attorney setting forth the terms and conditions of the retention and signed by the attorney, the claims person, and the insured. If the attorney or law firm has an ongoing relationship with the insurer, only the person being defended need sign an engagement letter.[1]

The engagement letter should, at least, list the following details:

- The effective date of the agreement.
- The fees to be charged, the units by which fees are calculated (usually in six minute increments or tenths of an hour) and a representation as to how often the attorney will submit fee bills (usually monthly or quarterly).
- A description of reasons for discharge and withdrawal, or conclusion of services.
- A disclaimer of guarantee.

It should also outline the scope of the engagement, i.e., specify that counsel will:

- Review copies of contracts and insurance-related documents he or she has been provided with.
- Review the files of the insurance broker and/or the underwriting files of the insurer.
- Attend, take, review, and analyze the deposition(s) of the plaintiff and defendant,

experts, and factual witnesses, as well as any other depositions agreed to be reasonably necessary.

- Review any other files or documents that counsel, the claims person, and the insured defendant deem necessary. These might include those of plaintiffs and defendants, as well as others.

- Review all pleadings and discovery that he or she, as well as the claims person and the defendant, deem necessary to present a competent defense.

- Provide his or her opinion regularly as the case progresses and respond to inquiries from the claims person and the insured defendant.

- Consult regularly with the insured defendant and the claims person on various issues related to the case.

- Prepare regular reports to the insured defendant and claims person.

- With the approval of the claims person, file necessary motions to the court, including a motion for summary judgment.

- If appropriate, attend mediation or settlement conferences with the insured defendant and claims person after providing the insured and the claims person with opinions on the settlement value of the case.

- If all attempts at settlement fail, present evidence at trial and defend the insured through trial and any necessary appeals.

At retention, the claims person should, in writing, instruct counsel on the following matters:

- the basic facts of the case learned in the initial investigation;

- a brief description of the documents collected by the adjuster;

- a statement of the date and time the summons and complaint were served on the insured;

- a summary of the coverage and limits available to the insured; and

- transcriptions of all recorded statements taken by the adjuster.

The adjuster should provide the attorney with as many original documents as possible and keep copies for his or her own files. All documents collected by the adjuster are important to the defense. This includes the service copy of the summons and complaint. The adjuster must advise the attorney of the exact date and time the complaint was served on the insured to ensure that a timely response is filed and to prevent the entry of a default. In most states a defendant has 30 days from the date the complaint is served to file a formal response (20 days in federal courts). Failure to formally respond to the complaint or obtain an extension of time to respond allows the plaintiff to declare the defendant in default and seek judgment as if the defendant had admitted all of the allegations of the complaint. Once a default has been entered, a judgment against the insured will follow unless good cause can be shown why the default should be set aside. Adjusters should make every effort to avoid putting an insured into such a difficult position by retaining counsel promptly. The insured must also report service of a lawsuit immediately with advice as to the time and place the summons was served, the person who received the summons, and the reason for any delay in delivery to the insurer.

The defense attorney should also have available:

- a specimen copy of the policy;

- a complete copy of the claim file; and

- a copy of the insurer's policy, if any, with regard to billing and case handling.

If the insurer's billing and case handling policies are not available in written form, the initial retention letter should describe them or it should be attached as an exhibit.

The adjuster and the attorney should meet in person to reach an agreement that they will work as a team in handling the case through trial.

Relationship between the Insurer and the Defense Attorney

Whenever an insured is sued and requires a defense or the insurer is sued, the insurance adjuster and the defense attorney must understand their respective roles in preparing the case for trial. They must develop a rapport with each other and with the insured person or entity that is being defended, to make communication easier to maintain. Bad faith lawsuits and poorly tried bodily injury cases seem to arise when the adjuster and the defense attorney fail to communicate regularly with each other.

At the first meeting, the attorney and the adjuster should agree on the division of labor with regard to the preparation of the case, according to their respective training and experience. Counsel and the claims person should reach an agreement regarding the handling of the case. Claims adjusters often mistakenly leave all investigation tasks to the attorney. Most adjusters are also investigators and are trained to fulfill the duties of an investigator within their narrow field of expertise. Therefore, the adjuster should do as many informal interviews of witnesses and parties as possible. The attorney should limit his or her investigation work to the preparation of witnesses before the trial or deposition.

Work that is usually done by the attorney or by a legal assistant includes:

- meeting with the insured to obtain facts for answering interrogatories;
- interviewing the insured and key witnesses, including getting recorded statements from each;
- collecting and preparing documentary evidence, such as medical records, police reports, and employment records;

- preparing for and taking depositions of parties (including plaintiff or defendant and independent witnesses);
- preparing written discovery such as interrogatories, requests for admission, and requests for production of documents; and
- preparing, filing, and arguing motions with the court.

Challenges to Use of House Counsel

Defense counsel are sometimes employees of the insurance company. Some attorneys have challenged the use of in-house counsel on the ground that the insurer, as an employer of attorneys, is not licensed to practice law. They claimed that the insurer was engaged in the unauthorized practice of law—a crime. Attorneys in Texas convinced a trial court on the issue but failed on appeal.

Attorneys have also raised challenges against house counsel because the employee attorney is alleged to be serving two different masters. As an employee of the insurer (it is alleged) the attorney cannot do justice to both his client, the insured, and his employer, the insurer.

A Texas court of appeal refused to limit the right of insurers to hire staff attorneys. In *American Home Assurance Company, Inc. v. Unauthorized Practice of Law Committee*, the court stated:

> American Home and Travelers may use staff attorneys to defend claims against insureds provided that the insurer's and insured's interests in the situation are congruent as described in this opinion, but staff attorneys must disclose their affiliation to their clients. [2] (Citations omitted.) Another Texas court concurred:

Use of staff attorneys to represent insureds is not the unauthorized practice of law. As [*Utilities Insurance Co. v. Montgomery*, 134 Tex. 640, 138 S.W.2d 1062 (1940),] pointed out, the insurance company in providing an attorney to the insured is "seeking to protect its own interests." Even though the attorney does represent the insured, the insurance company is not practicing law because of the company's direct financial interest in the litigation against the insured. There is no violation of Tex. Bus. Corp. Act Ann. art. 2.01B (2) because the purpose of an insurance company is to indemnify its insureds. The agreement to defend and pay attorney's fees is collateral to that purpose.[3]

Six of the state court decisions[4] have cited *Utilities Ins. Co. v. Montgomery*[5] as supporting the majority rule, even though *Montgomery* involved the use of outside counsel. Even *Gardner v. North Carolina State Bar*,[6] which held that the use of staff attorneys constitutes the unauthorized practice of law, pointed out that Texas has a special rule for insurance companies and cited *Montgomery*. In *Cincinnati Insurance Company v. Wills, 717 N.E.2d 151, 155–56 (Ind.1999)* the precise question was whether an insurance company engaged in the unauthorized practice of law when it employed house counsel to represent insureds. Specifically, the plaintiffs in Wills sought to disqualify the defendant's insurer from using house counsel, arguing that it amounted to the unauthorized practice of law. The court held first, that the use of house counsel to represent insureds did not necessarily amount to the unauthorized practice of law, and second, that in-house attorneys appearing as counsel to defend claims against an insured did not necessarily trigger an impermissible conflict in violation of the Rules of Professional Conduct. In reaching this holding, the court made several observations about the notice required to a policyholder regarding the possibility that house counsel may be used for claims defense. Evidence presented to the court that contended that State Farm either: a) delivered a product different than that promised in the policy (which stated clearly that it would provide counsel OF ITS CHOICE in the event of a lawsuit), or b) was unjustly enriched by its house counsel arrangement. As the Indiana Supreme Court noted in Wills, that stated that "[I]n the realm of insurance defense, the public may ultimately reap the benefits of better service at lower cost through the use of house counsel." This hardly sounds like the makings of a claim for unjust enrichment. [*Golden v. State Farm*, 745 F.3d 252 (2014)]

Reporting Requirements

The defense attorney should be required to report to the claims person and the insured defendant on a regular basis, and the adjuster should establish reporting requirements clearly with the attorney. Requirements should include, at a minimum:

- that the attorney report the progress of the case no less than every 60 days to the claims person and the insured even if the report states nothing new has occurred;

- that copies of all pleadings filed by both the attorney and his or her opponent be delivered to the adjuster and the insured;

  - that the attorney need send only one copy of each pleading to the adjuster and the insured, regardless of the number he or she may receive; and

- that with regard to answers to form or pattern interrogatories, requests for admission, requests for production of documents or other written discovery, and minor pleadings, such as demands for jury trial or notices of continuance, the attorney use his or her discretion as to whether to advise of their existence or to send copies to the adjuster and the insured.

If the case is complicated, or has multiple parties, the adjuster may wish to keep only a skeleton file of pleadings and discovery and obtain summaries of relevant pleadings and discovery from the attorney. Now that technology permits it, the attorney should be asked to avoid excessive use of paper documents and instead send copies of the documents, pleadings, discovery, and correspondence in electronic form.

Involvement of the Adjuster

At the moment the suit is assigned for defense the adjuster and the defense attorney must have a clear understanding of the adjuster's involvement in the preparation of the case for trial. The adjuster must make it absolutely clear that the attorney is required to abide by any guidelines provided by the insurer. If the attorney believes that the guidelines impinge on his or her ethical obligations, he or she will advise the adjuster, and they should work together to modify the guidelines appropriately.

The insurer's guidelines for case control and billing may change from time to time. The adjuster must keep abreast of such changes and promptly inform the attorney of them.

Control of the litigation process rests with the insurer who pays the fees. The insurer retains, and pays, the attorney to represent the insured defendant. The attorney is obligated to serve his or her clients, the insurer and the insured defendant(s), as they desire—as long as their instructions do not cause him or her to breach his or her professional ethics.

Despite the adjuster's prerogative to direct the attorney's handling of the case, the prudent adjuster will not prevent the defense attorney from doing work the attorney advises is necessary to properly defend the insured.

The adjuster and the attorney must meet regularly to review the file and discuss:

- further investigation;
- discovery needed; and
- any changes in the evaluation of the exposure the insured faces that have resulted from the work done by the attorney since the last meeting.

The case review meetings should take place no less than once every six months, and more frequently as the case comes closer to trial. The insured should be invited to attend and participate if the insured is able to attend. In addition to allowing the adjuster to become totally familiar with the case, the periodic case review sessions allow the adjuster, the attorney and the insured to get to know each other on a personal basis. This will allow the two to foster a mutual relationship of trust and respect that cannot be achieved with contact only by telephone, letter, e-mail, or fax.

After each case review the adjuster and counsel should agree on the terms and conditions of a report to the insured and insurer concerning the status of the case as discussed at the case review meeting.

In the last three months before trial these meetings may need to take place as often as every week. In the last days before trial it may be necessary for the adjuster, the attorney and the insured client to meet daily to properly prepare for trial.

Early Investigation

Initial Evaluation

The adjuster and the attorney should put together a reasonable evaluation of the damages that are recoverable by the plaintiff so that the adjuster can properly reserve the file with an estimate of the probability of the plaintiff recovering damages on the tort claim. The adjuster must provide information to the attorney regarding the specific items of damage that should be considered in the initial evaluation, including the following:

- past and future medical expenses;
- loss of earnings and earning capacity;
- loss of future earning capacity;
- physical and mental impairment;
- physical disfigurement;

- physical pain and suffering, including trouble and inconvenience caused by the incident;
- mental anguish;
- loss of consortium;
- emotional distress;
- loss of household services; and
- punitive damages sought (even though there is seldom insurance provided for such damages).

After the initial evaluation is completed a report should be prepared and delivered to the insurer and the insured defendant.

The Litigation Plan

It is useful to both the adjuster and the attorney if they work together to prepare and implement a litigation plan. The plan should include:

- an outline of the work that will be done on the case;
- a list of all discovery requirements and deadlines imposed by the court in the jurisdiction where the case is to be tried. This should include:
- the date the complaint must be answered;
- any discovery responses that may be required if served on the insured at the same time as the complaint;
- immediate discovery that defense counsel should do to learn the basics of the case being brought by the plaintiff;
- discovery and motion cut-off dates; and
- a determination of what informal discovery or investigation the adjuster should perform with the assistance and direction of the attorney.

The litigation plan, coupled with periodic case reviews, assures the adjuster of complete involvement in the case, and enables the adjuster to control the activities of the attorney with counsel's permission and agreement.

Although cost containment is important to every insurer, it would be counterproductive to contain defense costs to such an extent that a large judgment against the insured becomes a certainty. The litigation plan can also act as a cost containment device since the attorney will not have carte blanche to do unlimited legal work. Counsel must be able to prepare the case for trial sufficiently, yet without indulging in the over preparation— work done by the unfettered attorney, for no litigation purpose—that some insurers believe is prevalent today.

Many insurers have a standard litigation plan of action form that requires the adjuster and defense attorney to mutually agree upon a plan of action, sign the document, and keep copies in their respective files. If the insurer does not have such a form, the adjuster should create a plan. The adjuster can smooth the way forward by asking the attorney to write a letter to the adjuster summarizing the proposed litigation plan after their first meeting.

The litigation plan should be a flexible document that the insurer and counsel understand will need frequent revisions as pleadings are amended, discovery progresses, and new facts are determined. Each time the adjuster and the attorney meet on a case review, the litigation plan should be updated and revised to reflect the current situation. At each case review the adjuster and attorney should reevaluate the exposure faced by the insured to understand:

- the appropriate reserve for indemnity;
- additional investigation or discovery required to mount a proper defense (if any);
- necessary revisions to the litigation plan timetable;
- the discovery portion of the case and the protection of the claim file; and

- the potential for settlement.

Discovery should include gathering all relevant documents, such as medical records, business records, and any other pertinent paperwork that will be used as an exhibit at trial.

The insured should be kept involved and informed. The defense attorney and/or the adjuster should involve the insured in all discovery responses. It is the insured who must swear under oath to the response and who will be called upon to testify at trial. It is important, therefore, that the adjuster and counsel be careful to not put words in the insured's mouth that he or she would not be willing to testify to at trial. Some insureds are so trusting of their attorney and insurer that they will sign anything presented to them. It is the duty of the adjuster and defense attorney to protect the insured from the insureds naiveté in such situations. This requires, for example, that counsel, the adjuster, or a member of counsel's staff read aloud to the insured every interrogatory and answer and ascertain that he or she is ready and willing to swear to the truth of the answers. In my experience, some plaintiff's attorneys have been known to get their clients to sign multiple blank verification forms (documents that state that the insured has read the responses and swears under oath that they are true), so that when interrogatories (questions in writing posed by one party to another that must be answered under oath) are due, the attorney need only insert a date—thereby causing a client to swear under oath to a document he or she has never seen. If the attorney retained by the insurer uses such a technique, the adjuster must stop the practice or dismiss the attorney. A competent attorney will always ask a defendant for the basis of his or her answers to interrogatories or other discovery. If the proceedings reveal that the defendant is not cognizant of the answers, it will be embarrassing, and could destroy the defendant's credibility at trial. Similarly, defense counsel should question each plaintiff carefully concerning responses to written discovery and confirm that the answers are actually those of the plaintiff and not plaintiff's counsel.

Delegating Litigation Plan Components

Some larger law firms have found it effective to break up the work of trial preparation—depending on the complexity of the case—among various members of the firm. For example, an associate may be assigned to:

- do the initial drafting of pleadings;
  - do legal research on the issues raised by the pleadings;
- draft initial interrogatories and requests for admission; and
- take depositions of various witnesses.

A paralegal or legal assistant may be assigned to:

- collect documents;
- conduct initial meetings with the client/insured;
- begin drafting responses to interrogatories posed by the attorney for the plaintiff;
- help collect the documents the plaintiff's attorney has demanded from the client/insured;
- collect the plaintiff's medical records;
- prepare summaries of depositions;
- prepare draft answers to written discovery for submission to the attorney; and
- prepare summaries of documents collected.

The adjuster could be assigned to do the first four of these tasks in order to contain costs, if his or her caseload allows. The adjuster could also be assigned to obtain:

- recorded statements from each independent witness;
- inspections of the scene of the loss; and
- photographs, video footage, film, or other depiction of the scene of the loss.

The defense attorney will be required to establish the legal theories applicable to the case, evaluate the legal issues raised by the case, take the key depositions, and handle the actual trial. Smaller law firms without extensive staff may have the defense attorney do all the work except the investigation, which is left to the adjuster.

There is a debate in the insurance and legal community as to which method of trial preparation is most appropriate. I believe the insured client and the insurer are better served when the attorney who is designated to try the case does all of the preparation. In my experience, an attorney's familiarity with how a case is tried enables him or her to take a more informative deposition of a witness than someone with less – or no – experience in court. It may be more cost effective to the client to have a less experienced associate take discovery but the effort may prove more expensive at the time of judgment if the discovery is incomplete or inadequate.

Regardless of how the work is broken up, it is important to establish a timetable to establish when each task in the litigation plan is to be accomplished. The adjuster should also estimate, with the assistance of counsel, the cost of each phase so that the anticipated expenses are adequately reserved. Since most plaintiffs' lawyers work on a contingency fee basis they are incentivized to do as little work as possible at the early stages of a case hoping for a quick settlement and higher proportion of fees collected to the hours worked. Defense counsel, on the other hand, best serves his or her client by fully preparing the case for trial early – within the first six months – by taking all written discovery and necessary depositions before the plaintiffs' lawyer gets out of bed.

General Discovery

The key to civil litigation is discovery, the process whereby each party demands information from the other and is entitled to a fair response. *Black's Law Dictionary*[7] defines "discovery" as "compulsory disclosure, at a party's request, of information that relates to the litigation." If one party refuses to answer fully the inquiries of the other a court can, and usually will, compel responses. In the context of an insurance claim case, discovery should include:

- depositions; and
- written discovery, such as interrogatories, requests for statements of damages, requests for production of documents, and requests for admission.

It is helpful if the adjuster is involved in the discovery process rather than simply acting as the person granting authority to expend funds. The adjuster assists discovery by conducting formal recorded witness interviews and informal witness interviews. The adjuster's work assists counsel in preparing for depositions and in directing appropriate written discovery. If possible, the adjuster should attend depositions of important parties and witnesses to be fully informed and to be available to assist counsel.

A deposition is not a court proceeding and proceeds under rules different from those of a trial. For example, inquiry concerning hearsay or unauthenticated documents is permissible in a deposition, but not at trial. The scope of discovery is necessarily broader than proof at trial. It shall not be ground for objection that the information sought will be inadmissible at trial if the information sought appears reasonably calculated to lead to the discovery of admissible evidence. [*Fischer v. Ulysses Partners, LLC*, Not Reported in A.3d, 2016 WL 4543964 (2016)]

The Claim File

The claim file must accurately reflect everything performed by the claims personnel and be absolutely truthful. It should document each and every step of the investigation performed by the adjuster. Every word written in the claim file should be written as if the adjuster were speaking to a jury or would not be concerned if it was read to a jury. It can be extremely embarrassing if the contents of the claim file are made subject to discovery by the plaintiff and read to the jury at trial.[8]

Since the claim file is prepared by the insurer, not the defendant, it is usually not subject to discovery in a third party bodily injury or property damage case. In such a case almost all work done by the adjuster can be described as work done in anticipation of litigation, even if no suit has yet been filed, and thereby be inviolate as the work product of and for an attorney. In most jurisdictions, documents prepared in anticipation of litigation are protected from discovery under what is known as the attorney's work product protection (sometimes wrongly called the "work product privilege").[9] The purpose for this protection is to allow an attorney to prepare the case properly without worrying that opposing counsel will have access to this work to assist his or her own preparation for the case. To allow that to occur would obviously be unjust.

Courts have established a test to determine whether a document was prepared in anticipation of litigation. In order to protect the work from the plaintiff's prying eyes there must be:

- an objective examination of the facts surrounding the investigation;
- outward manifestations which indicate litigation is imminent; and
- evidence that shows whether the party opposing the discovery of the document had a good faith belief that litigation would ensue.

For example, in *Hickman v. Taylor*[10] the US Supreme Court concluded that:

> historically, a lawyer is an officer of the court and is bound to work for the advancement of justice while faithfully protecting the rightful interests of his clients. In performing his various duties, however, it is essential that a lawyer work with a certain degree of privacy, free from unnecessary intrusion by opposing parties and their counsel.... Proper preparation for trial requires that counsel assemble information, sift what counsel considers to be the relevant from the irrelevant facts, prepare legal theories, and plan strategy without undue and needless interference.

However, since there is always a possibility that a court will find that the work product protection does not apply, the adjuster should only write material in the claim file that he or she will be comfortable having read in open court. Many courts hold that routine work does not fall within the protection, such as when:

- the document is a standard form not used in litigation; or
- the document was prepared when there was no outward sign of litigation.

QBE *Insurance* sought to protect claim notes as attorney work product. The issue was whether or not those notes had been prepared in anticipation of litigation or for trial by or for another party or its representative under Federal Rule 26(b)(3)(A). Because all insurance investigations are likely performed with an eye toward the prospect of future litigation, it is particularly important that the party opposing production of the documents, on whom the burden of proof as to the protection rests, demonstrate by specific and competent evidence that the documents were created in anticipation of litigation. Other objective benchmarks relied upon by the federal courts bearing on the anticipation of litigation issue include the following:

(1)   whether the investigation is of a third-party claim, the very nature of which is anticipating litigation, or a first-party claim;

(2)   that insurer-authored documents are more likely than attorney-authored documents to have been prepared in the ordinary course of business;

(3)   that the work product doctrine most strongly protects the mental processes of the attorney, providing a privileged area in which to analyze and prepare a client's case as opposed to documents which consist of factual materials and analyses of facts;

(4)   that actions taken by an insurance company immediately after being notified of a potential claim are almost always part of its ordinary business of claim investigation; and

(5)   that blanket assertions of work product as to entire files, rather than specific documents are never sufficient to prevent discovery, since the party opposing discovery must establish that each document is work product. [*Hill v. Northland Cas. Col*, 2015 WL 6405764 (2015)]

Some courts have held that unless an investigation was made at the request or under the guidance of an attorney, the investigation must conclusively be presumed to have been made in the ordinary course of business.[11] Other courts hold that the involvement of an attorney is not determinative.[12] Some courts have recognized the truth of the matter—that almost all insurance investigations are in anticipation of litigation.[13]

The Iowa Supreme Court, affirming *Ashmead*, held that:

> Subject to the provisions of R.C.P. 125, a party may obtain discovery of documents and tangible things otherwise discoverable under subdivision (a) of this rule and prepared in anticipation of litigation or for trial by or for another party or by or for that other party's representative (including the party's attorney, consultant, surety, indemnitor, insurer, or agent) *only upon a showing that the party seeking discovery has substantial need of the materials in the preparation of the case and that the party seeking discovery is unable without undue hardship to obtain the substantial equivalent of the materials by other means.* In ordering discovery of such materials when the required showing has been made, *the court shall protect against disclosure of the mental impressions, conclusions, opinions, or legal theories of an attorney or other representative of a party concerning the litigation. Exotica Botanicals, Inc. v. E.I. Du Pont De Nemours & Company, Inc.*, No. 107/98-559 (Iowa 07/06/2000). (Emphasis added).

The Author

Barry Zalma is an insurance coverage consultant and Certified Fraud Examiner who now limits his practice to consultation, arbitration or mediation of insurance disputes. He is the founder of Barry Zalma, Inc., a California law firm whose practice emphasized the representation of insurers and those in the business of insurance.

Mr. Zalma is the author of many books, e-books, continuing education courses, and articles relating to insurance coverage, insurance claims handling and insurance litigation. His books and e-books on Insurance Claims, Construction Defects, Mold and Insurance Law are available ClaimSchool, Inc., The American Bar Association, Thompson Reuters, and Fastcase.com's Full Court Press. Details available at

He is an internationally recognized expert on insurance claims handling, insurance coverage, insurance fraud investigations, the commercial general liability policy, the comprehensive general liability policy, the homeowners policy, all first and third party insurance policies, inland marine coverages, and the tort of bad faith at http://zalma.com/blog/insurance-claims-library/